in his own words

£2·75

Neil Young

C000171772

Michael Heatley

OMNIBUS PRESS
London / New York / Sydney

Copyright © 1997 Omnibus Press
(A Division of Book Sales Limited)

Edited by Chris Charlesworth.
Cover & book designed by Michael Bell Design.
Picture research by Nikki Russell.

ISBN 0.7119.6161.1
Order No.OP47861
Visit Omnibus Press at http://www.musicsales.co.uk

Exclusive Distributors:
Book Sales Limited, 8/9 Frith Street, London W1V 5TZ, UK.
Music Sales Corporation, 257 Park Avenue South, New York, NY 10010, USA.
Music Sales Pty Limited, 120 Rothschild Avenue, Rosebery, NSW 2018, Australia.
To the Music Trade only:
Music Sales Limited, 8/9 Frith Street, London W1V 5TZ, UK.

Photo credits
Front cover: London Features International.
Richard Aaron/Star File: 75; Dagmar/Star File: 21; Max Goldstein/
Star File: 47; Harry Goodwin: 24b, 53c, 54, 55b, 61r; Bruce Gregory/Star File: 13;
Larry Kaplan/Star File: 34; London Features International: back cover insets,
4, 6, 7, 8, 10, 11t&b, 12, 14, 15, 16, 18, 19, 20t, 23c&b, 24t, 26, 29, 30, 31, 35, 37,
38, 39, 42, 45, 49, 50, 53b, 55t, 57, 58, 59, 60, 61L, 62, 63L, 64, 65, 66, 67, 68, 69,
70t&b, 71, 72, 73t&b, 77t&b, 78, 79, 80, 82, 85, 86, 89, 90, 92, 93, 94, 95, 96:
Jeffrey Mayer/Star File: 17, 32, 40, 81, 91; Al Pereira/Star File: 56, 74; Chuck Pulin/
Star File: 22, 52; Robert Teese/Star File: 28; Laurens Van Houten/Star File: 20b,
63r, 76; Barry Wentzell/Star File: 36.

Every effort has been made to trace the copyright holders of
the photographs in this book but one or two were unreachable.
We would be grateful if the photographers
concerned would contact us.

Printed in the United Kingdom by Page Bros.

A catalogue record for this book is available from the British Library.

Introduction

In an era of two-dimensional rock stars, Neil Young is unique.
He appeared at Woodstock, yet was untainted by peace and love
associations that saw contemporaries labelled 'Sixties throwbacks'
by a less tolerant generation. He was one quarter of a supergroup
in Crosby Stills Nash & Young, yet he retained his street
credibility – so much so that he was a crucial influence on Nirvana
grungemeister Kurt Cobain two decades later. He's cut pop, rock,
country, synth-rock, horn-led R&B... almost every genre you could
conceive, impressing every one with his own personal stamp to
turn a disparate selection of musical styles into a coherent whole.
In short, he's a one-off.

His own explanation of this scattershot musical philosophy is
endearing, if not revealing. "Every one of my records, to me, is like
an ongoing autobiography," he says, adding "I can't write the same
book every time." That view certainly struck no chords with David
Geffen, whose label sued Young for producing 'uncharacteristic'
material. Needless to say, there could only be one winner...

Surprisingly for a man who's most often associated with the
US West Coast scene, Young was born in Canada and remains a
Canadian citizen. That's never stopped him expressing his political
views, though, and his backing of Ronald Reagan was rivalled only
by Paul Weller's "I'm voting Conservative" admission at the height
of the New Wave. Like Weller, Young has always been a loose
cannon – and has often appeared to revel in it.

When it comes to drugs, Young – unlike President Clinton –
admits to inhaling. But his views have been tempered by the deaths
of musicians close to him, notably Crazy Horse guitarist Danny
Whitten, and the long-term crack problem of CSN&Y bandmate
David Crosby. Moreover, his domestic situation as father to two
handicapped kids has inspired him to take a wider world view than
those whose interests and perspectives begin and end with music.
Give Young a topic and he'll run with it – something that makes him
good copy and the ideal subject for this book, which brings together
three decades' worth of wit, wisdom and whimsy.

Young's music has rarely been less than compelling, whether solo,
with CSN&Y, Crazy Horse (his backing band for over a quarter of a
century) or shorter-lived aggregations like The Bluenotes. All in
all, he's not done badly for someone whose first record as a member
of Winnipeg's Squires back in 1963 was an instrumental because the
producer told him he couldn't sing. Then, as ever, Neil Young had
the last word.

Canada - A Way Of Life

Everybody in Canada wants to get to the States. At least they did then. I couldn't wait to get out of there because I knew my only chance to be heard was in the States. But I couldn't get down there without a work permit, and I didn't have one. So eventually I just came down illegally, and it took until 1970 for me to get a green card. I worked illegally during all of the Buffalo Springfield and some of Crosby Stills Nash & Young. I didn't have any papers.

I couldn't get a card because I would be replacing an American musician in the union. You had to be real well known and irreplaceable and a separate entity by yourself. So I got the card after I got that kind of stature – which you can't get without being there... the whole thing is ridiculous. The only way to get in is to be here. You can't be here unless it's all right for you to be here. It's like 'throw the witch in the water, and if it drowns it wasn't a witch. If it comes up, it is a witch, and then you kill it.' Same logic. But we finally got together. **1975**

Obviously there was more that happened in Winnipeg than happened in Toronto for me. But what happened in Toronto seemed to be more of a stepping stone. It was more of a transition. And when I went to LA, I came from Toronto: I didn't come from Winnipeg... that's where it all started for me, there's no doubt about that. That was where a lot of important things happened for me. 1987

Crosby Stills Nash & Young at Live Aid, 1985

I used to spend my time at school drawing amplifiers and stage set-ups. I wasn't into school. I was always flunking out. **1987**

I haven't changed citizenship because I think it could somehow be taken as a rejection of Canada. I figure I was born in Canada, therefore I'm a Canadian. 1992

Canada just couldn't support the ideas I had. The sounds I liked were coming from California. I knew that if I went down there I could take a shot at making it. **1994**

A lot of my songs come from flashes of things in my past. It's not specific but you'll get images here and there that are about Canada. 1994

Omemee, Ontario... It's where I first went to school and spent my 'formative' years. Actually, I was born in Toronto... 'I was born in Toronto'... God, that sounds like the first line of a Bruce Springsteen song. **1995**

Right after I left the Mynah Birds I took up as a solo folk singer. Come to think of it, I did a bit of that before the Mynah Birds also. After I arrived in Toronto I tried to keep my band going and then tried to work with several others. But it just never worked out for me there. I could never get anything going in Toronto, never even got one gig with a band. I just couldn't break into that scene. So I moved instead towards acoustic music and immediately became very introspective and musically-inward. That's the beginning of that whole side of my music. 1995

The Hawks were the best band in Toronto, which is the biggest city in Canada, musically. And I'd just come from a place called Thunder Bay which is between Winnipeg and Toronto. We'd done really well there but we couldn't get a gig to save our lives in Toronto. All we ever did was practise. So I ended up cruising around by myself on acoustic guitar, playing my songs at coffee houses for a while, just showing up at these places. It was quite an experience! I remember it now as... 'Wow, this is really out-on-the-edge!' Walking around in the middle of the night in the snow, wondering where to go next! **1994**

Family

My father played a little ukulele. It just happened. I felt it. I couldn't stop thinking about it. All of a sudden I wanted a guitar, and that was it. I started playing around the Winnipeg community clubs, high school dances. I played as much as I could... always with a band. I never tried it solo until I was 19. 1975

Of the two of them, my father was definitely more musically-oriented. Mom and Dad used to listen to the old big bands, Lena Horne, Della Reese, Tommy Dorsey, Glen Miller Orchestra, Cab Calloway... **1995**

Lena Horne

Dad wasn't living with me at the time, he didn't have the perspective my mother had. If he had, he'd have seen how 'into the music' I was, but at the same time he'd have been pushing me to stay on at school, just like my mother was. And I definitely think he'd have certainly been stronger at persuading me to stay on. But the classic thing that happens in family break-ups... the perspective gets changed.

The father will always have a negative reaction to what the mother does, particularly if she's being 'soft' on the child. Without the true understanding of what's going on, he'll just say that 'it's wrong'. It's a reaction created out of frustration over not being able to really voice an opinion. So... to say that my father was less into my music than my mother would be unfair. Although my mother was more supportive. 1995

Just why (my two sons) were born with cerebral palsy... there's no way to tell. My third child, Amber, is just a little flower, growing like a little flower should. It took (wife) Pegi a lot of preparation to get ready to have another kid because it was really hard for us to face the chance that things might not work out right. But so many doctors told us that it had nothing to do with anything. **1988**

With wife Pegi

I couldn't believe it. There were two different mothers. It couldn't have happened twice.

I remember looking at the sky, looking for a sign, wondering 'What the fuck's going on? Why are the kids in this situation? What the hell caused this? What did I do? There must be something wrong with me.'

So I made up my mind that I was going to take care of Pegi, take care of the kids. We were gonna go on, we weren't going to be selfish and I wasn't going to be hurt. I closed myself down so much that I was making it, doing great with *surviving* – but my soul was completely encased. I didn't even consider that I would need a soul to play my music, that when I shut the door on 'pain', I shut the door on my music. 1990

I've always felt that God made my son the way he is because he was trying to show me something, so I try to do as much positive as I can for people like that, and for families of kids who are handicapped. I have a lot of compassion for those people and a lot of understanding for them that I didn't have before, and I think it's made me a better person.

And I think since I have the power to influence so many people, it was only natural that I should be shown so many extremes of life, so I could reflect it somehow. **1985**

Ben is a great little guy, a wonderful little human being. He's got a really beautiful little face, and he's got a great heart, and he's a lot of fun to play with. We've got a train set that we play with, that he controls with buttons and stuff.

He's learning how to communicate and play games and solve problems using a computer. And he is handicapped in as much as he has severe cerebral palsy, and he is a quadriplegic, and he's a non-oral child. So he has a lot of handicaps. Cerebral palsy is a condition of life, not a disease. It's the way he is, the condition he's in. He was brought into the world in this form, and this is the way he is. A lot of the things that we take for granted, that we can do, he can't do. But his soul is there, and I'm sure he has an outlook on the world that we don't have because of the disabilities. 1988

My son Zeke has very mild cerebral palsy. He's a wonderful boy, and he's growing up to be a strong kid. He's going to be 16 in September, and one of the things he really wants to do now is get his driver's licence. He's a great guy, a great kid... **1988**

Often in my life I've felt that I was singled out for one reason or another for extreme things to happen. This was hard to deal with. We've been dealing with it, and we've learned to turn it around into a positive thing and to keep on going. It was something that brought Pegi and I really close together, just having the strength to have another child and having her be such a beautiful little girl and having everything work out. Just believing. Coming around to believing that it's okay for us to try again. 1988

There was a lot of pain, and I just withdrew. I cut myself off from virtually everything. I closed the door. You can only feel so much and then you have to deny it. You can't deal with it. That was a heavy thing for me. I dealt with it for a while, as best I could. But then I just had to cut myself off from everything. I just closed that door. And I was cut off from everything. Because, you know, what had happened was a real private thing. I couldn't share it…

No one knew what I was doing. Nobody could understand it. The record company was pissed off at me. Everybody was pissed off at me. **1990**

If I haven't written anything in a long time, I tell all the people who rely on me for a living that they should maybe start looking around. "I don't know if I'm gonna be there for you now," I tell 'em. It's not happening. But whenever I'm complacent about music or haven't anything to say, that's when I don't play. I've got my hobbies and I've got my family, things I share with my son, my daughter and my wife. My wife Pegi's my best friend and my lover. Together, we've had the wonderful feeling of bringing kids up, seeing them grow up.

The truth is, I was a lot older ten or 15 years ago than I am now. I had to work hard on it. 1995

The Early Bands

The Squires

The first song I ever sang in public was at Kelvin (High School) in the cafeteria. It was a Beatles song called 'Money, That's What I Want'. I think I was also working on 'It Won't Be Long'. **1987**

We were learning about the business and we were pretty naïve, but we had a lot of fun and hung out together a lot. 1987

There was somebody in somebody's garage or basement that recorded us. It was me and Ken Koblun, Randy Peterson and Doug Campbell. We made a record of a song called 'I'm A Man And I Can't Cry'. That was the first record of me singing. I had a copy of the tape for years but I don't know where it is now. We got a pretty good sound. That was a great group. If we'd played more shows, it would have been unbelievable. **1987**

I probably asked almost everybody in Winnipeg to go (on the road). I was trying to put together a band and I was looking for people who wanted to take a chance. Maybe that's why I couldn't find any. I think a lot of people wanted to go but couldn't. 1987

It was a constant uphill battle to get gigs. Finally, we decided if we wanted to get somewhere, we had to get out... (We chose Fort William) because it was halfway between Winnipeg and Toronto. We became really popular around that area. Because we weren't from Fort William, we were more interesting. We were a step above most of the Fort William bands because it was a smaller town, and we were from Winnipeg. **1987**

The Shadows

We were going that way (folk-rock). We had a lot of songs that we were doing in that period that were kind of arrangements of other songs. We got into a thing where we did classic folk songs with a rock'n'roll beat and changed the melody. We did a really weird version of 'Tom Dooley' which was like rock'n'roll but it was in minor keys. And then we did 'Oh! Susannah' based on the arrangement by a group called The Thorns: Tim Rose was in The Thorns. We saw them at the Fourth Dimension. And also we did 'Clementine' and 'She'll Be Coming Round The Mountain When She Comes'. I wrote all the new melodies. We changed them totally with rock'n'roll arrangements. It was pretty interesting. It was different. 1987

The Shadows became the major part of our repertoire. We did 'Apache', 'Wonderful Land', 'FBI' and 'Shindig', and another one called 'Spring Is Nearly Here'. **1994**

With Robbie Robertson and
Rick Danko of The Band at
The Last Waltz, The Band's
farewell concert in San Francisco,
1976

**I always believed I could find someone else who might have
the same determination I had. If somebody didn't fit in, I knew
I had to tell him to go. I had to shit on a lot of people and leave
a lot of friends behind to get where I am now, especially in the
beginning. I had almost no conscience for what I had to do.
There was no way that I could put up with things that were going
to stand in my way. I was so driven to make it.** 1994

In Fort William... we just got way out there and went berserk.
That was one of the first times I ever started transcending on guitar.
Things just got onto another plane. Afterwards people would say,
'What the hell was that?' That's when I started to realise that I had
the capacity to lose my mind playing music. **1994**

Buffalo Springfield

**Great experience. Those were the really good days. Great people.
Everybody in that group was a fucking genius at what they did.
That was a great group, man. There'll never be another Buffalo
Springfield. Never. Everybody's gone such separate ways now,
I don't know. If everybody showed up in one place at one time with
all the amps and everything, I'd love it. But I'd sure as hell hate
to have to get it together. I'd love to play with that band again,
just to see if the buzz was still there.** 1975

Bruce Palmer and I were tooling around LA in my hearse. I loved
the hearse. Six people could be getting high in the front and back,
and nobody would be able to see in because of the curtains.
The heater was great. And the tray... the tray was dynamite. You
open the side door, and the tray whips right out onto the sidewalk.
What could be cooler than that? What a way to make your entrance.
Anyway, Bruce Palmer and I were taking in California. The Promised
Land. We were heading up to San Francisco. Stephen and Richie Furay,
who were in town putting together a band, just happened to be
driving around, too. Stephen Stills had met me before and remembered
I had a hearse. As soon as he saw the Ontario plates, he knew it
was me. So they stopped us.

I was happy to see *anybody* I knew. And it seemed very logical to us that we form a band. We picked up Dewey Martin for the drums, which was my idea, four or five days later. Stephen was really pulling for Billy Mundi at the time. He'd say, 'Yeah, yeah, yeah. Dewey's good, but *Jesus*... he talks too much.' I was right, though, Dewey was good. **1975**

I think people really have that friction business out of hand. Stephen and I just play really good together. People can't comprehend that we both can play lead guitar in the band and not fight over it. We have total respect for musicianship, and we both bring out the perfectionist in each other. We're both very intense, but that's part of our relationship. We both enjoy that. It's part of doing what we do. In that respect, being at loggerheads has worked to our advantage. Stephen Stills and I have made some incredible music with each other. Especially in the Springfield. We were young. We had a lot of energy. 1975

I just couldn't handle it toward the end. My nerves couldn't handle
the trip. It wasn't me scheming on a solo career, it wasn't anything
but my nerves. Everything started to go too fucking fast, I can tell that
now. I was going crazy, you know, joining and quitting, and joining
again. I began to feel like I didn't have to answer or obey anyone.
I needed more space. That was a big problem in my head. So I'd quit,
then I'd come back 'cause it sounded so good. It was a constant
problem.

I just wasn't mature enough to deal with it. I was very young.
We were getting the shaft from every angle, and it seemed like we
were trying to make it so bad and were getting nowhere.
The following we had in the beginning, and those people know who
they are, was a real special thing. It gave all of us, I think, the strength
to do what we've done. With the *intensity* that we've been able to do
it. Those few people who were there in the beginning. **1975**

**We were young. We were all emotionally involved to the
point where we were still growing up. We didn't know what was
happening to us.** 1979

I played here once (Troy in upstate New York) with the Buffalo
Springfield. I remember we didn't get our money. The guy drew
a gun on us, told us to get the fuck out. Those were the good
old days. **1985**

Stephen Stills

There actually have been several Buffalo Springfield reunions in the last two years. At Stills's house. We just get together every couple of months and play. The original guys – Richie (Furay), Dewey (Martin), Bruce (Palmer), Stephen and I. We've done this three, maybe four times, and I'm sure we'll do it again. 1988

On a Buffalo Springfield reunion

I just can't see it. I mean, what would be the point? Buffalo Springfield are all part of the past now. If we reformed we'd be like a statue or something. A monument with pigeons shitting on our heads. And that just wouldn't be right. **1990**

We thought we were going to be together for about 15 years, because we knew how good it was. 1994

There were a lot of problems happening with the Springfield. There were a lot of distractions too. Groupies. Drugs. Then there were all these other people... They were always around, giving you grass, trying to sell you hippy clothes... I never knew what these people really wanted. And there were so many of 'em! Not to mention all the women... all the clubs, places to go, things to do. I remember being haunted suddenly by this whole obsession with "How do I fit in here? Do I like this?" **1994**

The first time I went to the Fillmore was with Buffalo Springfield in '66. We played The Rolling Stones show at the Hollywood Bowl and then got in a Lear jet and flew up to San Francisco from Burbank and played at the Fillmore the same night. I don't think we were very good. I think we were a little... LA. 1995

Actually, the reason I initially left the group was because I didn't want to do the *Johnny Carson Tonight Show*. I thought it was belittling what the Buffalo Springfield was doing. That audience wouldn't have understood us. We'd have been just a curiosity to them. **1995**

THE BUFFALO SPRINGFIELD ALBUMS

Buffalo Springfield 1967

On 'Burned'

My first vocal done in a studio, late 1966 (Gold Star). The boys gave me some uppers to get my nerves up. Maybe you can hear that. I was living in a $12.50 per week apartment at the time and everybody on the floor liked it too. We stayed up all night listening to it. 1977

The real core of the group was the three Canadians – me, Bruce Palmer and Dewey Martin. We played in such a way that the three of us were basically huddled together behind while Stills and Furay were always out front. 'Cos we'd get so into the groove of the thing, that's all we really cared about. But then we got into the studio and the groove just wasn't the same. And we couldn't figure out why. This was the major frustration for me as a young musician, it fucked me up so much. Buffalo Springfield should have been recorded live from the very beginning. **1994**

Buffalo Springfield Again 1967

On 'Expecting To Fly'

**It came from two or three songs that I moulded together
and changed around and fitted together. We spent three weeks
recording and mixing it. It's not a modern recording, it's based
on an old theory... blending all the instruments so they all sound
like a wall of sound.** 1969

On 'Broken Arrow'

It's an image of being very scared and mixed up. The broken arrow
is an Indian sign of peace after losing a war. A broken arrow usually
means that somebody has lost a lot.

Even back then I thought the way records were being made
in the 1960s was wrong. But I didn't know what was wrong with it.
It just didn't sound right. I mean, the Springfield records are *terrible*
compared to what The Band sounded like. **1992**

Last Time Around 1968

**The last real album that Buffalo Springfield made was 'Buffalo
Springfield Again'. 'Last Time Round' was pieced together by Jim
Messina because neither Steve nor I gave a shit... we just didn't
want to do it, y'know. It's weird.** 1969

On 'I Am A Child'

The group was falling apart by this time. We all cooked separately
in the studios. The Sunset Sound receptionist's boyfriend is on bass.
The rest is me. **1977**

Solo

**I needed to get out to the sticks for a while and just relax.
I headed for Topanga Canyon and got myself together. I bought a
big house that overlooked the whole canyon. I eventually got out
of that house because I couldn't handle all the people who kept
coming up all the time. Sure was a comfortable fucking place...
that was '69, about when I started living with my first wife, Susan.
Beautiful woman.** 1975

I started working on my own record right away. Couldn't get off
Atlantic (Records, the Springfield's label) fast enough; I mean, only
because I wanted to be separate from the Springfield. I didn't want to
be competing with other members on the same label. **1980**

**I see country music, I see people who take care of their own.
You got 75 year old guys on the road. That's what I was put here
to do y'know, so I wanna make sure I surround myself with people
who are gonna take care of me. 'Cos I'm in it for the long run.
Willie Nelson's 54 years old and he's a happy man, doing what he
loves to do. I can't think of one rock'n'roller like that. So what am
I gonna do?** 1985

Willie Nelson

I didn't go away! I just did other things. But I didn't go away, OK!
I'm not like some Sixties band coming back to take advantage of some
wave of bullshit nostalgia.

My whole career is based on systematic destruction. See, that's
what keeps me alive. You destroy what you did before and you're free
to carry on... And now... Now I'm just fine!

All I'm saying is... All these reviewers writing stuff about my
comeback... I don't have to come back because I've never been gone!
They write stuff like "Oh, this year Neil Young's OK again." I don't
need them to tell me if I'm OK or not. As far as I'm concerned, I've
always been OK.

With Keith Richards at the 1986 Rock and Roll Hall Of Fame ceremony in New York

I just can't associate with anyone or anything involved in a comeback right now. Well, sure, I can associate with Bob Dylan and Lou Reed. Both their recent albums are great. But with us three, you've got to understand – it's a big time in our lives right now. We've come through, we've survived intact and we're still creatively focused. But I can't – and I won't – relate myself to The Who or the Stones or The Jefferson Airplane. Not in the Nineties! No way. And I used to love all those bands, particularly the Stones. Only somewhere along the line they lost it for me. And then what happened in 1989 with those mega-tours – that was nothing more than a remembrance, a swansong.

The music the Stones and The Who play now has got nothing whatsoever to do with rock'n'roll. Spiritually it's all Perry Como. **1990**

I want to be able to see the people I'm playing for and I want the people to feel that the music is being made just for them – you bounce off people that way, get up, jump around, have a good time, get drunk – at least let's see each other, I've been right through that trip of massive audiences and my ego has been satisfied. I guess I had to do it... but once you've done it, then what? You realise that's not what communicating's all about.

When an over-zealous fan interrupted his flow, Neil lectured the audience at the Beacon Theater in New York about the relationship between the past and the present:

Y'know, every song was new once. When I first came to New York, I played at the Bitter End and at Carnegie Hall and I was playing as many new songs as I am now. The people who love me don't realise they're trying to stop me from going ahead. **1984**

None of those records was meant as a joke. I was deadly serious about what I was doing 'cos I desperately need to do something. But at the same time thru' most of the Eighties I didn't want my most innermost feelings about life and everything to come out.

The Who

Back then I had a lot of dark thoughts weighing on my mind
tied into the experiences that happened in my immediate family.
Things happened to me over those years I had no possible reason
or way to expect or capacity to explain. And it took me a long
time to get over it and come to terms with my life to date.
For better or worse, *Eldorado*, *Freedom* and *Ragged Glory* are
the result. 1990

The Albums

Neil Young 1969

I've remixed it and it's being remastered and reissued so that
people will be able to hear it properly. And I'm working out some
sort of deal with the record company so that the people who bought
it originally will be able to take it into a record shop and exchange
it for a new copy.

It took me and Jack Nitzsche a month to put down the tracks
for 'Old Laughing Lady'. I write in spasms – I did most of the songs for
the second album in one month, and after something like that I won't
write anything for weeks and weeks, maybe.

We did a lot of work on the first album – everything was
overdubbed to get that breadth of sound. But I really like to record
naturally. I'd rather put the voice down at the same time as the
backing tracks. **1970**

Very few of my albums are love songs to anyone. Music is so big,
man, it just takes up a lot of room. I've dedicated my life to my
music so far. And every time I've let it slip and gotten somewhere
else, it's showed. Music lasts... a lot longer than relationships do.
My first album was very much a first album. I wanted to prove to
myself that I could do it. And I did, thanks to the wonder of modern
machinery. That first album was overdub city. It's still one of my
favourites, though. 1975

'Sugar Mountain' single 1969

I do 'Sugar Mountain' really for the people more than I do it
for myself. I think I owe it to them, cos it seems to really make them
feel happy, so that's why I do that. They pay a lotta money to come
and see me and I lay a lotta things on 'em that they've never heard
before, and I think I owe it to them to do things they can really
identify with.

It's such a friendly song, and the older I get and the older my
audience gets the more relevant it becomes, especially since they've
been singing it for 20 years. It really means a lot to them, so I like to
give 'em the chance to enjoy that moment. I had it on the B-side of
almost every single that I had out for 10 years. **1985**

Harvest 1972

Most records I do, if I have the material done, it doesn't take very long for me to do it. *Harvest* was basically four sessions. There was the London Symphony Orchestra session, and then the session I did in Nashville during an acoustic tour I was doing at the time. I went back after the tour for another session and then I did a session at my barn. That was *Harvest*. 1993

I was in and out of hospitals for the two years between *After The Goldrush* and *Harvest*. I have one weak side and all the muscles slipped on me. My discs slipped. I couldn't hold my guitar up. That's why I sat down on my whole solo tour. I couldn't move around too well, so I laid low for a long time on the ranch and just didn't have any contact, you know. I wore a brace. Crosby would come up to see how I was; we'd go for a walk, and it took me 45 minutes to get to the studio, which is only 400 yards from the house. I could only stand up for four hours a day.

I recorded most of *Harvest* in a brace. That's a lot of the reason it's such a mellow album. I couldn't physically play an electric guitar. 'Are You Ready For The Country', 'Alabama' and 'Words' were all done after I had the operation. The doctors were starting to talk about wheelchairs and shit, so I had some discs removed. But for the most part, I spent two years flat on my back. I had a lot of time to think about what had happened to me. **1975**

With Graham Nash

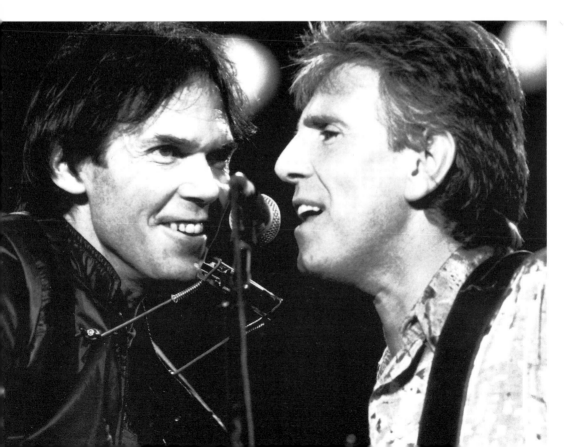

I realised this wasn't going to be the most satisfying thing, just sitting around basking in the glory of having a hit record, so I think I subconsciously set out to destroy that, before it surrounded me. 1992

A mellow trip, where my life was at the time; but only for a couple of months. It was probably the finest record I ever made – but that's really a restricting adjective for me. **1993**

On 'Heart Of Gold'

We went into the studio to cut the album, and I guess we were hot that night and it was a good cut but it's gone now. I've seen a few artists who've got hung up on the singles market when they've really been albums people... It's easy to do, but if you're wise, you stay with being what you really are... I just hope there is not a single on my next album. 1973

This song put me in the middle of the road. Travelling there soon became a bore so I headed for the ditch. A rougher ride, but I saw more interesting people there. **1977**

Time Fades Away 1973

Danny (Whitten)'s death... happened right before the 'Time Fades Away' tour. He was supposed to be in the group. We were rehearsing with him and he just couldn't cut it. He couldn't remember anything. He was too out of it. Too far gone. I had to tell him to go back to LA. "It's not happening, man. You're not together enough." He just said, "I've got nowhere else to go, man. How am I gonna tell my friends?" And he split. That *night* the coroner called me and told me he'd ODed. That blew my mind. Fucking blew my mind. I loved Danny. I felt responsible. And from there, I had to go right out on this huge tour of huge arenas. I was very nervous and... insecure. 1975

Time Fades Away was a very nervous album. And that's exactly where I was at on the tour. If you ever sat down and listened to my records, there'd be a place for it in there. Not that you'd go there every time you wanted to enjoy some music, but if you're on the trip it's important. Every one of my records, to me, is like an ongoing autobiography. I can't write the same book every time. There are artists that can. They put out three or four albums every year, and everything fucking sounds the same... **1977**

That isn't my trip. My trip is to express what's on my mind. I don't expect people to listen to my music all the time. Sometimes it's too intense. If you're gonna put a record on at 11.00 in the morning, don't put on 'Tonight's The Night'. Put on The Doobie Brothers. 1975

I imagine I could have come up with the perfect follow-up album
(to *Harvest*). A real winner. But it would have been something that
everybody was expecting. And when it got there they would have
thought that they understood what I was all about, and that would
have been it for me. I would have painted myself in the corner.
The fact is I'm not that lone, laid-back figure with a guitar. I'm just not
that way anymore. I don't want to feel like people expect me to
be in a certain way.

Nobody expected *Time Fades Away*, and I'm not sorry I put it
out. I didn't need the money, I didn't need the fame. You gotta keep
changing. Shirts, old ladies, whatever. I'd rather keep changing and
lose a lot of people along the way. If that's the price, I'll pay it. I don't
give a shit if my audience is a hundred or a hundred million. It doesn't
make any difference to me. I'm convinced that what sells and what
I do are two completely different things. If they meet, it's coincidence.
I just appreciate the freedom to put out an album like *Tonight's The
Night* if I want to.

**It makes you feel uneasy to listen to it. The only redeeming
factor was that it truly reflected where I was at. It was a chapter
that I wish hadn't been written but I knew I had to get it out
because I knew it represented something... Some people have
come up to me and said I love that record... but not many.** 1988

Comes A Time 1978

I was going one way and then needed to move in entirely the opposite direction just for some kind of 'release'. My career is built around a pattern that just keeps repeating itself over and over again. There's nothing surprising about it at all. My changes are as easy to predict as the sun coming up and down. **1995**

Decade 1977

We didn't put any of *Time Fades Away* on *Decade*. See, *Decade's* good for that reason. It makes a statement about my work from my point of view. Things were added in abundance and omitted. There's different angles in there. It's not like an even editorial. 1995

Hawks And Doves 1980

It's what you might call a transitional album for me. But that's not to say there aren't some really interesting things on there. 'Comin' Apart At Every Nail' is good, and I really like 'Union Man'. It's no big thing: just a funky little record that represents where I was and what I was doing at that time. **1995**

Trans 1983

I love the machines, and I think the machines are where it's at... I'll be able to completely disguise myself. Computer music, I think it's going to be my future. Although it may not be... 1982

Trans resulted from a fascination with machines and computers taking over our lives. This image of elevators with digital numbers changing and people going up and down the floors – you know, people changing levels all under the control of a machine. And drum machines, the whole thing. And here I was, like an old hippie out in the woods, with all this electronic equipment. I mean, I was astonished. I had a whole video thing in mind for that record. I had characters and images of beings that went with all the voices. But I could never get anybody to make the videos. I could never get anybody to believe that the idea was any good. **1988**

If you listen to *Trans*, if you listen to the words to 'Transformer Man' and 'Computer Age' and 'We R In Control', you'll hear a lot of references to my son and to people trying to live a life by pressing buttons, trying to control the things around them, and talking with people who can't talk, using computer voices and things like that. It's a subtle thing, but it's right there. But it has to do with a part of my life that practically no-one can relate to. So my music, which is a reflection of my inner self, became something that nobody could relate to. And then I started hiding in styles, just putting little clues in there as to what was really on my mind. I just didn't want to openly share all this stuff in songs that said exactly what I wanted to say in a voice so loud everyone could hear it. 1988

My son is severely handicapped, and at that time was simply trying to find a way to talk, to communicate with other people. That's what *Trans* is all about. And that's why, on that record, you know I'm saying something but you can't understand what it is. Well, that's the exact same feeling I was getting from my son.

I don't underrate *Trans*. I really like it, and think if anything is wrong, then it's down to the mixing. We had a lot of technical problems on that record, but the content of the record is great. **1995**

Everybody's Rockin' 1983

That was as good as *Tonight's The Night* as far as I'm concerned. The character was strong, the story was great but unfortunately, the story never got to appear on the album. Before I got a chance to finish it – I got stopped from recording. Geffen cancelled a couple of sessions where I was going to do two songs – 'Get Gone' and 'Don't Take Your Love Away From Me' – that would've given a lot more depth... But if you didn't see the shows you wouldn't be able to get into it fully. Of course, it wasn't anywhere near as intense as *Tonight's The Night*. There was very little depth to the material obviously. They were all 'surface' songs. But see, there was a time when music was like that, when all pop stars were like that. And it was good music, really good music.

See, when I made albums like *Everybody's Rockin'* and everyone takes the shit out of 'em... I knew they could do that. What am I? Stupid? Did people really think I put that out thinking it was the greatest fuckin' thing I'd ever recorded? Obviously I'm aware it's not. Plus it was a way of further destroying what I'd already set up. Without doing that, I wouldn't be able to do what I'm doing now. If I build something up, I have to systematically tear it right down before people decide, "Oh, that's how we can define him." 1995

Old Ways 1985

There are a lot of science fiction overtones, time travel overtones, in 'Misfits'. People at different places geographically, it could all have been happening at exactly the same time. All of the scenes in that song could have been happening simultaneously, and yet they're also separate. It's an interesting thing…

It only took me a few minutes to write it. I picked up my electric guitar one night in the studio, I was by myself and I turned it up real loud and started playing, and I wrote it just that night. Just got into it. Jotted it down on a piece of paper. **1985**

Landing On Water 1986

That album was like a rebirth, just me coming back to LA after having been secluded for so long. I was finding my rock'n'roll roots again. And my vibrancy as a musician. Something came alive; it was like a bear waking up. 1988

Eldorado 1989

On the limited availability

If somebody really wants to hear it, they can always go ahead and make a copy of it. This is the digital age. Go ahead, make a copy. I don't care. **1989**

I recorded a lot of stuff, eight or nine songs, at the Hit Factory in New York on *Times Square*. And I put together an album called *Times Square*, and then I changed the name to *Eldorado*.

**And then I mastered it and then just as it was being readied
for release I changed my mind about it because I thought I really
wanted to have an album that was really gonna make an effect.
That wasn't just gonna be something I wanted to do. I decided
that I'd done what I wanted to do long enough and just wasn't
doing that enough. I thought *Eldorado* by itself was a really fine
album, but, you know, if you don't have a record they can play on
the radio, you might as well forget it. You might as well not put
out a record. So I took the songs that really created the feeling of
Eldorado and put them out as an EP, therefore eliminating any
of the crap that I have to go through by not even entering the
arena.**

**At least I didn't have to put myself through this
exasperating experience of trying to get something I felt was
really me on the radio only to find out over and over again that
no one's gonna play it because it doesn't fit with some format.
I'm sick of that.** 1990

Freedom 1989

I just wanted this one to be a Neil Young album, as silly as that
sounds for me to say. For years now I've skirted the issue of what was
really on my mind by doing stylistic things, genre albums. I wasn't
ready to talk about what had happened in my own life so I just shut
that all off. I'm coming out of that now but I alienated a lot of fans
by doing that too. Still, I had a hell of a good time doing it and you
only live once.

I worry all the time about how my stuff will be but I don't *care*
about it. Perhaps I should have made more movies and got it out that
way. Maybe if I'd have had enough offers to act in films, I might not
have made any records in the last ten years. But this record is just me;
it's what I think, what I feel. **1989**

On 'Rockin' In The Free World'

**The song itself is a lot of images and drugs and war and all
these Muslims hating us, Americans and Europeans alike. They're
not what we term 'civilised', and they think that we are barbarians,
we're like the devil to them. I'm just describing both sides like a
journalist. I mean, I don't have an opinion; there's no answer from
me, no guidance. I just write what I think I see and I change my
own mind about it every day...**

**The song is a similar thing to 'Born In The USA'. The chorus
cuts both ways. First, it's true – keep on rockin' in the free world,
that's what we Americans want to do, to keep on doing what we're
doing and moving forward. But then, how free is the free world
anyway? The Chinese students have this idealistic view of what
freedom and democracy are and they want it. I'm just saying.
Let's take a closer look.** 1989

Harvest Moon 1992

It's not less aggressive than my other three country records, but there's a peacefulness to it. After the war of *Weld* and *Arc*, there's just a time to go the other way, to go inside. It's almost like being in the eye of the storm. You're surrounded by energy, and yet everything's so quiet and peaceful. **1992**

I think the album is saying that it's okay that some things don't last forever. It doesn't mean you have to stop living or loving or experiencing things. You can still be as bright and into things as you were when you were young. It doesn't matter if you're 20, 30 or 40, whatever. The idea is to keep living. Don't snuff yourself out. 1992

I don't want to go back. My responsibility is to be here now, doing what I'm doing. I'm not yearning for the past, and that's not what *Harvest Moon* is about. Even as I get older I don't look back too much. I'm pretty happy with what I've got going now. All those things we all went through in the Sixties were great.

But I don't need them to happen again. What's gone is gone. You can't keep looking over your shoulder. If you keep thinking about the past and what might have been, you might as well live in a museum. **1992**

(It's) a more female record than any I've done. I think women who probably didn't like the last two will like it. It's a feminine record, and I wanted that element to keep on coming back. That's the point of this record. 1993

It's an album of songs about hanging on and trying to make things last, and being able to reach back into the past and take it with you, rather than having to abandon it. **1994**

I made *Harvest Moon* because I didn't want to hear any loud sounds. I still have a little bit of tinnitus but fortunately now I'm not as sensitive to loud sounds as I was for a year after the mixing of *Weld*. My hearing's not perfect but it's OK. I'm not sure what's going on but the point is I can still hear well enough to get off on what I'm doing. There's still a lot of detail I can pick up. I'm a fanatic for hearing detail and that's not been lost, tho' I've got these other sounds I have to deal with too. 1995

Mirrorball 1995

I don't like to go in the studio and work on just one song. Some people work for months on one song but I think I'd go nuts. I wanted to try and get more. So I just started thinking about them, who they were and who I was and we tried four songs – got three the first day and one the second day. Left. Booked two more separate days and got three more the first day. I had no songs, just ideas.

For the second day, I was writing the songs the night before and on the morning of the session. They were there, though. Sometimes I have to do that to myself to jar it loose...

There was no direction. There was not one word spoken to do with, y'know, You play here, you play there, let's do this, let's do that. Nothin' Not one word. We just started off, I'd play a little bit on the guitar and show them the changes and then play it and sing it and by the fourth time, it was over. **1995**

It's just a bunch of images that came out – and that's why I like the name *Mirrorball*, because it's a bunch of little squares or rectangular mirrors and you look in and it's a different thing in every one of 'em and it's twirling around. That's sort of what's happening with the record. That's how I rationalise it anyway.

If things are planned out too much and everybody knows what's going on and what's gonna happen, there's almost no reason to do it then, is there? 1995

I had this part in 'Peace And Love' but I couldn't find out how it fit. So I put on the guitar and turned the amp up real loud so no-one could hear me whispering to myself while I'm singing this thing and I started in and I played 'Downtown' for the first time and I was going, 'What the hell is this? It's a completely different groove!' There I was thinking, 'What am I gonna do with this song?' and the music just told me, 'Forget thinking. Music isn't thinking,' and literally I wrote the song right there in as long as it takes to play it. **1995**

Onstage with Pearl Jam

Pearl Jam recorded 'Act Of Love' on a DAT machine when Crazy Horse and I played it at the Hall of Fame thing. The next day they told me that they liked that one. 'Do you know it?' I asked and they asked about this one chord and then said, 'Sure, we know it.' After we played it together, Eddie (Vedder) and I were talking and he said, 'I think the guys would really like to record that song with you.' I just said, 'Well, that's great; let's set a time up. All I know is we ought to get it while it's hot. I mean we already missed it; the first time we did it live on stage at Constitution Hall was really good...' It was a refreshing change of pace for me. Nothing to stay on top of, I was nobody's boss – it was just fine. 1995

Recording *Mirrorball* was like *audio vérité*, just a snapshot of what's happening. Sometimes I didn't know who was playing. I was just conscious of this big smouldering mass of sound.

The whole record was recorded in four days and all the songs, barring 'Song X' and 'Act Of Love', were written in that four-day stretch. I played 'Act Of Love' with Crazy Horse in January at the Rock'n'Roll Hall of Fame. Then, the following night, I played it with Pearl Jam at a Pro-Choice benefit concert and the version was so powerful I decided there and then to record it with them as soon as possible. On a purely musical level, this is the first time I've been in a band with three potential lead guitarists since the Buffalo Springfield. **1995**

Crosby, Stills, Nash & Young

When the Springfield broke up, I felt I couldn't work in a group context and I certainly never realised I'd be in a group with Steve again, even though I guessed we'd probably be playing together sometime.

Now I think I've reached just about the perfect state. I'm part of the group, which I really dig, and I can also express myself as an individual through my own things. And I need very badly to make my own music, partly because it boosts my ego to the required dimension… **1970**

I love playing with the other guys, but playing with Stephen is special. David is an excellent rhythm guitarist, and Graham sings so great… shit, I don't have to tell anybody those guys are phenomenal. I knew it would be fun. I didn't have to be out front. I could lay back. It didn't have to be me all the time. They were a big group, and it was easy for me. I could still work double time with Crazy Horse. With CSN&Y, I was basically just an instrumentalist that sang a couple of songs with them. It was easy. And the music was great.

People always refer to me as Neil Young of CSN&Y, right? It's not my main trip. It's something that I do every once in a while. 1975

Everybody always concentrates on this whole thing that we fight all the time among each other. That's a load of shit. They don't know what the fuck they're talking about. It's all rumours. When the four of us are together, it's real intense. When you're dealing with any four totally different people who all have ideas on how to do one thing, it gets steamy. And we love it, man. We're having a great time. **1975**

Opposite:
Crosby Stills Nash & Young in 1969 with drummer Dallas Taylor (right)

Crosby Stills Nash & Young, 1974

When Stephen came up to the house and asked me if I'd play with them, I knew they must have needed me for something. I guess it was the live part where they didn't have enough electric guitars and rock and roll to maintain over the folk harmony thing. When I first joined the group they didn't want to use my name, they just wanted it to be Crosby, Stills and Nash. I thought, "Well, what's in it for me?" Eventually they saw the point, that it should be "and Young" on the end.

In that group I was always like an add-on. Even when we played live, I didn't come out at first, I came out later on, which in some ways was good for me. It separated me. I didn't really want to be grouped in with a bunch of other people. 1979

David says that he loves to play music with Crosby Stills Nash & Young more than anything in the world. I told them when they could prove that to me that that's really what he wanted to do with his life and give up drugs, that I would go out with them. I told them that three years ago, and it hasn't happened yet.

The way I look at it, either he's going to OD and die or we're going to play together sometime. It's pretty simple. But until one of those things happens, until he cleans up, I'm not gonna do it. Live Aid was an exception to the rule which I made up on the spot. They all know how I feel.

I will not go out with CSN&Y, have everyone scrutinise the band, how big it is and how much it meant, and see this guy that's so fucked up on drugs, and who's not really so fucked up that he can't come back because we've all seen him when he's been clean recently, where he's very sharp just like he always was. So, y'know, until he has more respect for life and his effects on the young people… why should some young person who loves CSN&Y's old records from listening to their parents play them, some young kid 12 years old, why should he see CSN&Y on TV and know that this guy's a cocaine addict, been freebasing for fuckin' years and years and years, and he looks like a vegetable but they're still on TV and they're still making it and they're still big stars? I don't wanna show anybody that. That's something no-one should see. **1985**

There's a certain energy you get from singing with people you've known for twenty-five years. People who have been through all these changes with you. Gone up and down with you. Seen you do things that are wrong and seen you do things that are brilliant. Seen you fucked up to the max, you know? And you've seen them do all these things. And yet we're still here. Just to hear what it sounds like when we sing together after all these years – I was curious. I've wanted to do it for the last two or three years. And now it's possible.

I think that CSN&Y has a lot to say. Especially Crosby. His presence is very strong. Him being strong and surviving and writing great songs and being part of a winner is really a good role model for a lot of people in the same boat.

He's doing fine. His emotions are slightly shattered, because he's just abused his emotions for so long by not letting them out. But now that he's pure and can let his emotions out, his highs are real high, and his lows are real low. Those are just the extremes of his personality. But he pulls out of his lows, and they don't turn him toward any problem areas or anything. 1988

We (Neil and Stephen) are like brothers, you know? We love each other, and we hate each other. We resent each other, but we love playing together. I see and hear so much in Stephen that I'm frustrated when it isn't on record or something, There have been a lot of frustrations through our whole lives with each other, but there's also been a lot of great music. He continuously blows my mind with the ideas that he has for my songs. He's one of the greatest musicians I've ever met in my life. Great singer, incredible songwriter. **1988**

Nash is a very straight, very sincere kind of organised guy, dedicated to quality and very reliable. And he's an extremely good singer. Amazing pitch. He likes to be on top of it. He takes a lot of pride in being totally able to accomplish whatever it is that has to be done. Without Nash, there would be no Crosby, Stills & Nash at all. It would have been over a long time ago. 1988

There's no way getting around the fact that a CSN&Y tour would be a nostalgia tour to a great degree. CSN&Y is Woodstock – it's that era, that whole generation so why go out there and not be at our physical best? If people are looking at us as their brothers who they went through all these changes with, do they want to see somebody who's not together? No, they want to see someone who's super strong, who's endured, who's a survivor and is still creative and looks better than ever.

    If we go out there and fall on our ass, what are we? Dean Martin? All the alcoholics who went to see him, they didn't say, "Wow, look at Dean. He used to drink so much, but he got himself together and now he's strong, up there with Frank and Sammy." I feel sorry for the guy. **1988**

Stills is definitely the rowdiest of the four of us, as far as abuses and things like that. But he's at a time in his life when things are real important. He's just been married, and his wife's pregnant. There are a lot of new things happening. And he and I playing together is a nice resurgence. 1988

The Albums

Déja Vu 1970

The band sessions on that record were 'Helpless', 'Woodstock' and 'Almost Cut My Hair'. That was Crosby, Stills, Nash and Young. All the other ones were combinations, records that were done by more than one person using the other people. 'Woodstock' was a great record at first. It was a *great* live record, man. Everyone played and sang at once. Stephen sang the shit out of it. The track was magic.

Then, later on, they were in the studio for a long time and started nitpicking. Sure enough, Stephen erased the vocal and put another one on that wasn't nearly as incredible. They did a lot of things over again that I thought were more raw and vital-sounding. But that's all personal taste. I'm only saying that because it might be interesting to some people how we put that album together. I'm happy with every one of the things I've recorded for them. They turned out really fine. I certainly don't hold any grudges. **1975**

'Ohio' single 1970

It's still hard to believe I had to write this song. It's still ironic that I capitalised on the death of these American students. Probably the biggest lesson learned at an American place of learning. 1977

'American Dream'

We tried to make a good album, and it turned out to be okay. I think it's over, y'know. It's not exciting. **1989**

You'd have thought our performance on Live Aid would have been enough to finish off any wave of nostalgia, wouldn't you? Seriously though, I think CSN&Y reminds people of a certain feeling. Our audience want to see it alive again because somehow it verifies the feeling that they're alive too. CSN&Y – when it works – can make music that is very committed, heartfelt and sincere. It's not easy to get it out and it's not easy to overcome some of the bullshit around it. *American Dream* was an attempt that failed to reach anything like its true potential. But that's no reason for me to not try it again sometime. 1995

Crazy Horse

Crazy Horse bring out a part of me that's very primitive. We really put out a lot of emotion – which is easy for a kid to relate to. So it's very childlike. I've had some great times with Crazy Horse. 1988

I'm oversimplifying, but you could compare CSN&Y to The Beatles and Crazy Horse to the Stones. With Crazy Horse, I'm trying to make records that are not necessarily hits, but which people will listen to for a long time. **1969**

Billy Talbot is a massive bass player who only plays two or three notes. People are still trying to figure out whether it's because he only *knows* two or three notes or whether those are the only notes he wants to play. But when he hits a note, that note speaks for itself. It's a big motherfucking note. Even the soft one is big... Without Crazy Horse playing so big, I sound just normal. But they supply the big so I can float around and sound *huge*'. 1988

I love to do that kind of music. That's the most natural thing for me, playing with Crazy Horse. But it's not everything and right now it's not enough. Plus I can only play the way I play with Crazy Horse occasionally these days. **1990**

It's always great when I play with Crazy Horse because there's a kind of Zen drive there. I'm lucky because I'm just following the trail here. If something comes along that feels good and creative and makes me want to write more songs, then I'll do that. Every time I make a change, I can feel the repercussions of it. Obviously, there are people whose lives are directly affected when I make decisions to play with different bands but I have to live with that; I couldn't be guilty about it. I have to follow the vision of where the music is taking me. 1995

Albums

Everybody Knows This Is Nowhere 1969

Everybody Knows This Is Nowhere is probably my best (album). It's my favourite one. I've always loved Crazy Horse from the first time I heard The Rockets album on White Whale. The original band we had in '69 and '70 – Molina, Talbot, Whitten and me. That was *wonderful*. And it's back that way again now. Everything I've ever done with Crazy Horse has been incredible. Just for the *feeling*, if nothing else. **1975**

Where it comes from originally is... Stills and I on 'Bluebird'. We discovered this D modal tuning at around the same time in '66,

I think... We'd play in that tuning together a lot. This was when 'ragas' were happening and D modal made it possible to have that 'droning' sound going on all the time, that's where it started. Only I took it to the next level which is how 'The Loner' and 'Cinnamon Girl' happened. You make a traditional chord shape and any finger that doesn't work, you just lift it up and let the string just ring. I've used that tuning throughout my career right up to today. 1995

After The Goldrush 1970

In all modesty, *After The Goldrush*, which was kind of the turning point, was a strong album. I really think it was. A lot of hard work went into it. Everything was there. The picture it painted was a strong one. *After The Goldrush* was the spirit of Topanga Canyon. It seemed like I realised that I'd gotten somewhere. I joined CSN&Y and was still working a lot with Crazy Horse... I was playing all the time. And having a great time. Right after that album, I left the house. It was a good coda. **1975**

I remember thinking that *Goldrush* was the next logical step after *Everybody*. Just after I'd begun playing with CSN&Y, I went out on the road and did some really funky things that indicated that our next album would be in that particular vein. We recorded 'Wondering', 'Dance Dance, Dance', 'It Might Have Been', 'Winterlong' and several others. Things were moving very quickly at that time so it's hard to say... exactly why I went for *Goldrush* instead of that project. 1995

Tonight's The Night 1975

I'm really turned on by the new music I'm making now, back with Crazy Horse. Today, even as I'm talking, the songs are running through my head. I'm excited. I think everything I've done is valid or else I wouldn't have released it, but I do realise the last three albums have been a certain way. I know I've gotten a lot of bad publicity for them. Somehow I feel like I've surfaced out of some kind of murk. And the proof will be in my next album. *Tonight's The Night*, I would say, is the final chapter of a period I went through. **1975**

I would have to say that's the most liquid album I've ever made. You almost need a life preserver to get through that one. We were all leaning on the ol' cactus... and, again, I think that it's something people should hear. They should hear what the artist sounds like under all circumstances if they want to get a complete portrait. Everybody gets fucked up, man. Everybody gets fucked up sooner or later. You're just pretending if you don't let your music get as liquid as you are when you're really high. 1975

Tonight's The Night is like an OD letter. The whole thing is about
life, dope and death. When we played that music we were all thinking
of Danny Whitten and Bruce Berry, two close members of our unit lost
to junk overdoses. The *Tonight's The Night* sessions were the first time
what was left of Crazy Horse had gotten together since Danny died.
It was up to us to get the strength together among us to fill the hole
he left. The other OD, Bruce Berry, was CSN&Y's roadie for a long time.
His brother Ken runs Studio Instrument Rentals, where we recorded
the album. So we had a lot of vibes going for us.

There was a lot of spirit in the music we made... I probably *feel*
this album more than anything else I've ever done. **1975**

**I only had nine songs, so I set the whole thing aside and did
On The Beach instead. It took Elliot (Roberts, manager) to finish
Tonight's The Night. You see, a while back there were people who
were gonna make a Broadway show out of the story of Bruce Berry
and everything. They even had a script written. We were putting
together a tape for them, and in the process of listening back on
the old tracks, Elliot found three even older songs that related to
the trip, 'Lookout Joe', 'Borrowed Tune' and 'Come On Baby Let's Go
Downtown', a live track from when I played the Fillmore East with
Crazy Horse. Danny even sings lead on that one. Elliot added those
songs to the original nine and sequenced them all into a cohesive
story. But I still had no plans whatsoever to release it. I already had
another new album called *Homegrown* in the can.**

**I had a playback party for *Homegrown*. We all listened to the
album, and *Tonight's The Night* happened to be on the same reel.
By listening to those two albums back to back at the party, I started
to see the weaknesses in *Homegrown*. I took *Tonight's The Night*
because of its overall strength in performance and feeling.
The theme may be a little depressing, but the general feeling is
much more elevating than *Homegrown*. Putting this album out is
almost an experiment. I fully expect some of the most determinedly
worst reviews I've ever had.** 1975

I think this is one of my strongest and longest lasting albums.
It covers my obsession with the ups and downs of the drug culture.
Coincidentally it was my least commercially successful record ever.
1977

Zuma 1975
**I think I'll call it (the new album) *My Old Neighbourhood*.
Either that or *Ride My Llama*. It's weird, I've got all these songs
about Peru, the Aztecs and the Incas. Time travel stuff. We've got
one song called 'Marlon Brando, John Ehrlichman, Pocahontas
And Me'. I'm playing a lot of electric guitar, and that's what I like
best. Two guitars, bass and drums. And it's really flying off the
ground, too. Fucking unbelievable. I've got a bet with Elliot that
it'll be out before the end of September. After that we'll probably
go out on a fall tour of 3,000 seaters. Me and Crazy Horse again.
I couldn't be happier.** 1975

On recording 'Cortez The Killer'

There was a power-cut in the recording studio. They missed a whole
verse, a whole section! You can hear the splice on the recording where
we stop and start again. It's a messy edit.

It was a total accident. But that's how I see my best art, as one
magical accident after another. That's what is so incredible. You see,
with lyrics I try not to edit anything. I just let it all come through.
I actually believe that if it was meant to be written down in the first
place, it has a place there. I only ever edit at all after I've actually
performed a song live. And I like to record 'em fast. Record 'em
quickly and move on to the next batch. **1990**

**It was a combination of imagination and knowledge.
What 'Cortez' represented to me is the explorer with two sides,
one benevolent, the other utterly ruthless. I mean, look at
Columbus! Everyone now knows he was less than great. And he
wasn't even there first. It always makes me question all these
other so-called 'icons'.** 1995

'Don't Cry No Tears' was one of the first 30 or 40 songs I
(ever) wrote. Oh yeah, there were a lot of them from back then.
Unfortunately, we only have 'glimmers' of most of them but we
do have actual recordings of five of them... I really love these
tracks, by the way. I'm not embarrassed by them or anything because
I'm so young. I mean, some of them I wanted to hear over and
over again, whereas others were clearly not successful. I think it's
real interesting when you hear the 'bad' ones with the good ones...
1995

American Stars'N'Bars 1977

Originally the concept was to have two sides on the album.
One was going to be American history and the other was going to be
American social comment – the bar culture where I was, at the time –
you know, drunk on my ass in bars. I couldn't remember the American
history part so we left that out. **1979**

Rust Never Sleeps 1979

I don't take it so seriously as before. When you look back at the old bands they're just not that funny. People want to be funny now, they want to have a good time. That's why the punk thing is so good and healthy... mostly the old rock'n'roll groups are just taking themselves too seriously. It's like they know they're human and they're going to die pretty soon and they're all falling apart... People want a star to be flashy and they want something they don't have to relate to as being human... Stars are supposed to represent something else... bigger than life. It's better to burn out than to fade away or rust 'cause it makes a bigger flash in the sky.

**   I can relate to *Rust Never Sleeps*. It relates to my career. The longer I keep going, the more I have to fight this corrosion. Now it's gotten to be like the World Series for me. The competition's there – whether I will corrode and eventually not be able to move anymore and just repeat myself, or whether I will be able to expand and keep the corrosion down a little.** 1980

Most of the songs of that album had been written well before The Sex Pistols were ever heard of. 'The Thrasher' was pretty much about me writing about my experiences with Crosby Stills & Nash in the mid-Seventies. Do you know Lynyrd Skynyrd almost ended up recording 'Powderfinger' before my version came out? We sent them an early demo of it because they wanted to do one of my songs. **1995**

Live Rust 1979

**The first album to come out (*Rust Never Sleeps*) was all new
songs, which was to give people an even break if they didn't want
to buy the soundtrack album which is going to have maybe ten
old songs on it. I don't like to repeat that over and over and say
that if you want to buy these new songs you've got to buy these
old songs. If they don't want to hear the old songs again they
don't have to buy it (*Live Rust*) to hear the new ones. That's why
I did that...**

Re-Ac-Tor 1981

We didn't spend as much time recording *Re-Ac-Tor* as we should've.
The life of both that record and the one after it – *Trans* – were sucked
up by the regime we'd committed ourselves to. See, we were involved
in this programme with my young son Ben for 18 months which
consumed between 15 and 18 hours of every day we had. It was just
all-encompassing and it had a direct effect on the music of *Re-Ac-Tor*
and *Trans*. **1995**

Arc 1991

**Back home, my wife Pegi works with this charity art fair.
She and her girlfriends set up this pancake breakfast at the art
fair and they get out there and usually blast The Rolling Stones at
six o'clock in the morning while people are eating and setting up
their art booths. And their's is the loudest booth in the place.
It's basically a bunch of girls who've had something to drink early
in the morning. They're playing the Stones, serving pancakes,
screaming, ringing bells.**

    **Well, I gave Pegi a copy of *Arc* and said, "Take this down and
put it on right away". And I was thinking that later on I'd find out
how long it lasted. It lasted a minute and a half. And then it was
gone. They couldn't take it all.** 1991

There is an order to it. I took 57 pieces that we called 'sparks'.
We took them out, numbered them and disassociated them from
the concerts that they came from. Of those 57 pieces, I chose 37.
I had them all on a database and I had all the keys and the lyrics
that were in each piece all written down, and the location of the
piece so I could tell what hall it was from, so that I could move
from one hall to another so the sound wouldn't change so
radically. **1991**

**It's refreshing. It clears the palate. Because of the fact that
there's no beat. It's not an insult to your sensitivity in what kind
of a groove you dig. There is no groove. Fuck that!** 1991

Weld 1991

There's nothing short enough on *Weld* to get played on the radio,
as far as I can tell. Even the songs people know, the endings are so
fucking long they can't play 'em. A song like 'Cinnamon Girl' –
we ruined it for the chance of being on the radio.

But for us, it was cool. We did what we wanted to do. **1991**

**I blew my head off during that tour. When we were playing
that stuff, it was intense. It was real. I could see people dying in
my mind. I could see bombs falling, buildings collapsing on families.
We were watching CNN all the time, watching all this shit happen,
and then going out to play, singing these songs about conflict.
It was a hard thing. And I feel there was nothing else I could do.
As soon as the war started, I changed the set list. A few 'Ragged
Glory' songs were replaced with older songs I knew people could
relate to. I knew people would be unified. Whatever could bring
people together was more important than me playing a new song.
We couldn't go out there and just be entertainment. It would
have been bad taste.** 1991

The song ('Blowin' In The Wind') itself asks the same questions
everyone was asking then about how long it will be before people
can be free. What do you have to do? What about the Palestinians?
They're embroiled in this thing. They're not free. The history of that
part of the world is so complicated I don't even understand it.
Now all we have is public opinion based on the latest thing we've
seen the Israeli soldiers do on television. It really should be a lot
deeper than that.

There was no other choice for me. That was the song. I just
had to do it. I didn't have the idea until we were out there practising,
getting ready for the show and the war was about to happen.
Then when it happened, I woke up one morning and said, "Well,
we're gonna do 'Blowin' In The Wind'." That'll get people's attention.
It will let them know what the show is about.' **1991**

Sleeps With Angels 1994

'Sleeps With Angels' has a lot of overtones to it, from different situations that were described in it. A lot of sad scenes, I've never really spoken about why I made that album. I don't want to start now. 1995

Stills-Young Band

Telegram to Stills from Young on leaving the Stills-Young Band tour:

Dear Stephen, funny how things that start spontaneously end that way. Eat a peach. Neil. **1976**

I was having a pretty good time, but the reviews were playing us off against each other. Stephen was reading the reviews, I was trying not to read the reviews. But even the headlines were... well, like 'Young's hot, Stills not'. Then Stephen started thinking that other people on the tour were against him, trying to make him look bad... 1976

The Bluenotes

On the '87 Crazy Horse tour, The Bluenotes are born...

Every night I'd listen and the acoustic set didn't move me very much and the Crazy Horse set I'd just skim through because it seemed a little obvious. But that little blues set I did with Crazy Horse and our roadie on the baritone sax, well, I liked listening to that. I'd listen to every song all the way through. I'd listen to every note. It was kind of a lounge sound and it was cool and I really dug it and the crowd seemed to like it too 'cos they were going nuts and no-one was shouting for 'Southern Man' like they'd do in the acoustic set – like they've done throughout my career. So I decided what the hell is going on here, man? This is really wild. I've got to do something with this blues shit and stuff... It wasn't really blues you know, but it was *blue* and it was swinging and I had to do it...

I decided I wanted to make a movie about a blues band. I'm going to tell a success story about these guys who are not young guys, they're just regular family guys who all have jobs and who play this bluesy lounge music together and all of a sudden it starts to be pretty good. This band, The Bluenotes, are not fashionable and they are not cool and they're not hip and there's no scene around them. That was the movie I had in my head. But then I thought, if I'm really going to do this, I'll have to get a band for real – get some characters and some horns and make it really swing and try it out on the road. So that little movie in my head evolved into The Bluenotes and we're playing the clubs and the movie will come later... **1988**

We kicked around the idea of doing some old Buffalo Springfield songs like 'On The Way Home' or 'Mr Soul' so that it would give people a kind of reference point for how long this music has been a part of my life, so that it kind of ties The Bluenotes into another thing. But I don't know if I'm going to do that or not. I might if I go out and play bigger places. 1988

The blues is a vehicle for me to play in that I really enjoy. There seems to be a lot of emotional expression there for me in that style and I'm always happy when that's there. **1988**

The Album

This Note's For You 1988

I don't think it's really blues. It's blue. It's blues-influenced. I'm not trying to say that all of a sudden I'm a blues musician and that's all. I shy away from trying to say that I'm a blues musician or anything. I'm just playing this kind of music because I like it... It's kind of rhythm'n'blues, but there's also something original going on there in songs like 'Hey Hey'. 1988

There's things happening on that record that haven't happened on other records. Three of the songs have a late-night, torch-song kind of sound. You know, the club's-empty kind of feeling. We're getting ready to do the videos for The Bluenotes album and it will look like an empty club with one or two people there. **1988**

It looks like the record might be a hit. We hope it's a success. You know it's a ten-man band. It's not like having three guys like Crazy Horse. It's three times as expensive keeping this band going. 1988

Influences –
On Him & From Him

I've known Joni (Mitchell) since I was 18. I met her in one of
the coffee houses. She was beautiful. That was my first impression.
She was real frail and wispy-looking. And her cheekbones were so
beautifully shaped. I remember thinking that if you blew hard enough,
you could probably knock her over. She could hold up a Martin D18
pretty well, though. What an incredible talent she is. She writes about
her relationships so much more vividly than I do. I use… I guess I put
more of a veil over what I'm talking about. **1975**

I got into a Dylan thing in grade nine, playing folk. 1987

Randy Bachman (Guess Who, BTO) was definitely the biggest
influence on me in the city. He was the best. Back in those days he
was years ahead of anybody else in the city. He was playing an orange
Gretsch, like this one I've got now, and I got one like his. **1987**

**Green On Red? Did they do one of my songs? Who was it did
'Like A Hurricane'? The Mission? Are they a huge band? When people
say a band are huge, I never know what to think. Musical Youth
were a huge band, hahaha. They were gigantic. All over 300 pounds
right, hahaha. When people sound like me I don't know what to
think because, you see, I don't listen very much.** 1988

Bob Dylan

Years ago – '62 maybe – I saw Roy Orbison in Winnipeg, saw
him all over the place that year. Got to talk to him once outside a gig.
He was coming out of his motor-home with his backing band, The
Candymen. That had a profound effect on my life. I always loved Roy.
I looked up to the way he was, admired the way he handled himself.

With Joni Mitchell

That aloofness he had influenced me profoundly. It was the way he carried himself, y'know, with his benign dignity… His music was always more important than the media. It wasn't a fashion statement. It wasn't about being in the right place at the right time making the right moves. That didn't matter to Roy. Just like it doesn't matter to me.

Anyway I've always put a piece of Roy Orbison on every album I've made. His influence is on so many of my songs… I've even had his photograph on the sleeve of *Tonight's The Night* for no reason, really. Just recognising his presence. There's a big Orbison tribute song on *Eldorado* called 'Don't Cry'. That's totally me under the Roy Orbison… spell. When I wrote it and recorded it I was thinking 'Roy Orbison meets trash metal' (laughs)… Seriously. **1990**

On 'The Bridge' tribute album to him

I love the record now. Before, I saw it as all these groups saying 'OK Uncle Neil, time for that rocking chair'. I love all those guys on that record – The Pixies, Sonic Youth and that Nick Cave guy in particular. When I heard it, it really touched me. 1990

I love The Rolling Stones. Did they play the Paradiso (in Amsterdam) and broadcast it in the park? That's a good concept. They should do that in London, outside Wembley or wherever it is. Now that they've done that big thing, they should really play the small places so that people who really wanna see the Stones can see 'em. They should do it for themselves, so they remember what it's like to play. They don't need that big shit any more. **1995**

I met Pearl Jam two or three years ago on tour. It wasn't just they were good, I could relate to what I would do if I was playing with them. And I could see myself doing it. The music worked. It had this drive. There's this big machine in there. I like that power. 1995

The Rolling Stones

When I was growing up, I remember guys like Frankie Laine. See, around the same time as Elvis, there was also *Rawhide* and all that cowboy stuff. I loved that stuff – I even covered one of his songs on the *Old Ways* album. 'The Wayward Wind'. It was one of his biggest hits up in Canada. See, I used to walk by a railroad track on my way to school every day. There was even a real 'hobo's shack' there. The song and the image have always stayed with me. When I hear it, I always think of being five or six, walking past that old shack and the railroad tracks gleaming in the sun and on my way to school every day with my little transistor radio up to my ear.

Another song from that period that I loved, and also ended up doing a version of with Crazy Horse and Jack Nitzsche on piano – it's a country waltz called 'It Might Have Been' recorded by Jo London. It was a big hit in Canada though it didn't mean anything in the States. Great record. Real, real soulful rendition. Unfortunately on my version, I screwed up almost all the words. **1995**

Kurt Cobain

Roy Orbison

I'd been into Dylan since '63 when I heard his very first album; that left a big impression on me. And later, The Byrds were great. What they did was deeply 'cool'. They really impressed me. 1995

They've started calling me Don Grungeone. I kinda got this fatherly thing happening right now. Don't ask me why. I'm just here, where I always was, doing what I love to do. **1995**

Miles (Davis) and (John) Coltrane, they're two of my favourites. My guitar improvisations with Crazy Horse are very, very Coltrane-influenced. I'm particularly taken by work like 'Equinox' and 'My Favourite Things'. Miles I love just because of his overall attitude towards the concept of 'creation', which is one of constant change. There's no reason to stay there once you've done it. You could stay for the rest of your life and it would become like a regular job. 1995

Kurt Cobain really, really inspired me. He was so great. Wonderful. One of the best, but more than that. Kurt was one of the absolute best of all time for me. **1995**

Songwriting

I started off writing instrumentals. Words came much later. My idol at the time was Hank B Marvin, Cliff Richard's guitar player in The Shadows. He was the hero of all the guitar players around Winnipeg at the time. Randy Bachman, too; he was around then, playing the same circuit. He had a great sound. Used to use a tape repeat. 1975

I try not to think about the songs that I write, I just try to write them. And I try not to edit them… I know there's a source where music comes through you and words come through you, and editing is really uh, something you do to something that you've thought about. If you think about it and you try to put it down, then you can edit it. If you're not thinking about it, you just open up and let it come through you, then editing it is… taking a lot of liberties.

I'm not sure that everything I write is mine. That's the difference.

I think some of the things I write are mine, but I think some of it just comes through me. My mind is working behind the scenes and puts these things together without me consciously thinking of it, and then when the time is right it all comes out. That's more like creation in the true sense of the word than it is a contrivance. I try not to worry about what people are gonna think about it till after I've recorded it and it's too late to change it. Then I'll start worrying about it. But then it's too late…

Sometimes I write first thing in the mornings. There's no rules. A lotta times I write driving vehicles or moving in vehicles, with no instruments, and I'll write the whole song and remember it all and know exactly what the music is before I even pick up an instrument. The whole thing, it just falls into place. **1985**

The time between 'Everybody's Rockin'' and 'Old Ways' was a longer period than Buffalo Springfield or CSN&Y was together. I still wrote a lotta songs in that period, I wrote two and a half albums' worth of material, so really I have a lot of stuff in the can that's been recorded, and a few songs that haven't been recorded. 1985

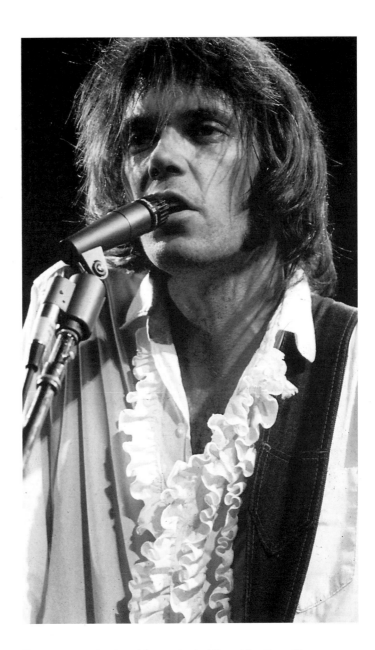

To me, my creation is not from a logical thought pattern; it's
from a sub-dominant hemisphere of the brain. It's from another place.
When I'm really writing; really playing, I'm not thinking at all. **1987**

**I've written most of my best songs driving on a long journey
scribbling lyrics on cigarette packets whilst steering.** 1990

It's pretty easy (being a prolific songwriter). Just as long as I don't try.
1995

Guitars & Guitarists

My first guitar was a Harmony Monterey acoustic with a pickup on it. 1987

I love Hendrix and the way he plays guitar. Nobody can play like that and nobody else ever will. **1988**

I am a naturally very destructive person. As a guitar player... that's where you get to hear how destructive I really am in my life. Man, if you think of guitar playing in terms of boxing... well let's just say I'm not the kind of guitarist you'd want to play against. 1990

I think origins are real important. I don't know who Jimi (Hendrix)'s roots were but he ended up sounding so great. As soon as he touched it, it was amazing. But he's hearing something, he's hearing it. That's why his thumb comes down the way it does, that's why he used finger picks or no picks or whatever, y'know, because he heard a certain sound. And the fatness and the distortion of the thing. He heard of it because of who he listened to. He formulated this sound in his mind probably from listening to BB King and Robert Johnson and all these Leadbelly kinda things.

When Jimi's first records came over, me and Jack Nitzsche listened to them over and over again. Y'know, "Wow! What the hell is this? This is great!" He's my favourite. Jimi and JJ Cale. Jimi and JJ got that feel. They can be real light with the guitar and there's that airy thing that happens that sounds so big and so good, so controlled and natural. **1995**

J.J. Cale
Jimi Hendrix

Hank Marvin

I listened to Hank Marvin. Back in the early days of The Shadows, he had a hell of a guitar sound. Who else? D'you remember at the very beginning, when Steppenwolf first came out, they had a guitar player in there, I think his name was Dennis Edmonton? He was, like, *bad!* Telecaster, distorted, slinky. And Link Wray. And Wes Montgomery... 1995

My first (guitar) was this little plastic Arthur Godfrey ukulele, then I seem to remember a baritone 'uke', then I had a banjo. So I had all these different-sounding instruments which I played the same way. I played electric lead guitar first. Then I started rocking out in a community-club teenage band. First we were called The Esquires. Then we changed it to The Stardusters. And after that we settled on being called The Squires. Kinda like Spinal Tap's early days! **1995**

Stephen Stills was a really great singer. He had the beginnings of being an electric guitar player too. Somehow we could play lead guitar parts simultaneously and not get in each other's way. And that's real rare. It gave the sound a real edge. And it has absolutely nothing to do with what he does by himself and what I do by myself. 1995

The Music Business

I think in some ways – only in some ways, but in some ways –
rock'n'roll has let me down. It really doesn't leave you a way to grow
old gracefully and continue to work.

If you're gonna rock you better burn out, cos that's the way
they wanna see you. They wanna see you right on the edge where
you're glowing, right on the living edge, which is where young people
are. They're discovering themselves, and rock'n'roll is young people's
music. I think that's a reality, and I still love rock'n'roll and I love to
play the songs in my set that are sort of rock'n'roll, but I don't see
a future for me there. **1985**

**I think there's a lot more to the world than fashion television
(MTV)... I was mellower when I was 24. I get angry at the world
a little bit these days. I get angry at things. This corporate
sponsorship thing just sneaked up on me and it bothered me
seeing it everywhere. I don't see what place it really has in music.
With music there should be a bond between performer and audience
and that really doesn't need a middle man; it doesn't need a
sponsor. I won't sign with some beer company because it's
misleading and deceitful, but unfortunately it's a very effective
thing and I'm just trying to call attention to it.**

**Millions and millions of dollars are spent on sponsorship
by these beer companies and Pepsi Cola, so I'm sort of going on
the offensive a little bit. It bothers me. I'd like to see them build
a Michelob or Budweiser centre for the homeless in New York.
They could make a building and fill it up with equipment and
everything for taking care of homeless people on a tiny percentage
of their sponsorship and advertising budget. I don't know... 1988**

There's a line, one of the first fucking lines that's ever been drawn where pop stars really have to show their stuff, show where they're really coming from. I mean, if you're going to sing for a product, then you're singing for money. Period. That's it. Money is what you want, and this is how you get it. **1988**

Reprise is really doing a great job of supporting me. They were willing to take me on my own terms and not tell me what kind of music to play. I have the freedom to do whatever I want. 1988

Well the context (of rock) changed because of MTV and the rock video. That's really it. Because by MTV trying to visualise the music they automatically stripped it of most of its natural mystery and depth. Before rock video, when people were confronted with the music, they had to rely on natural ability to utilise their own imagination… If they weren't also opting for some kind of state of enhancement via some drug or another.

Today in America, for better or for worse, rock'n'roll is Guns N'Roses. People call them evil but they're just kids. At least they were. You've just got to remember that it's the kids that made Guns N'Roses what they are, not Guns N'Roses making the kids what they are today. **1990**

With analogue recording, the moment used to be captured. When they got digital they concentrated on removing all the flaws, and forgot about preserving the sound. You can reproduce it and it never loses its quality; the only problem is, it never had quality in the first place. 1994

It's not a macho display like, y'know, some bands have this strutting thing where they get up there and move around and they sweat and they pose and they need to work out just to be in shape to go through all that. I mean, those guys are in great shape!

But the sweating we do is because we're so far into it that we've forgotten how to not sweat. Y'know, I'm thinking about the breathing and everything. I start hyperventilating, my nose gets really cold and I feel this cool breeze blowing in my face when it's about 110 on stage. It's like you just get to that point where nothing else is there, it's just all gone and you're taking off and everybody is way into it and then the whole crowd goes with you.

You see, in the Sixties, that used to happen a lot. That's what music was all about. Every band would jam on everything and the crowds would go berserk. I don't mean they were yelling for hits. I mean they just became a mass and they were lost in the music. It was truly an idealistic kind of musical experience.

And I think that happens more today than has happened in the last 25 years, because of this movement and Nirvana and Sonic Youth and related bands like that who have come along and made a big turn away from the mainstream while retaining all the values of pop music. It started turning all of it on the establishment. All this pessimistic music that says, "You created it, now listen to it", y'know? And now people are hearing it.

It makes a lot of sense to me to do it the way they're doing it. Now people go to a show and people are listening and they're playing and it's one thing. It's a bond that's consistent with the Sixties... Or maybe I just don't have any fucking idea at all what's going on and this has been fine for years and everybody was doing this!

The Sex Pistols, they were getting together, right, and everybody was into it and I didn't notice and I just woke up from a big dream. **1995**

What I'm really happy about is that I can see people relating to people who are singing directly to them and they feel the same way about things, about the commercialisation of their world and everything being sold before it's even finished and everything being kinda out of control and that their dreams probably won't come true as opposed to, in the Sixties, everybody's dreams were gonna come true, y'know, eventually. But here, these kids, they know. You can go all the way through school and not get a job. You can do all these things but things that we used to rely on are not there. 1995

The problems with celebrity and rock'n'roll start with the fact that nowadays it gets way too big too fast. Back in the Fifties and Sixties, rock'n'roll was 'big' but it was only 'big' to people who cared about it. Not it's big to people who don't care about it. So they can't begin to understand it. They just make ill-informed judgements on performers without first comprehending why or what it was that made the person famous in the first place.

In the Sixties there was a bond between the artists and the audience. It's harder to see now because so much these days is simply down to image projection. But today's pessimistic bands have a vision and an attitude that's unified their generation just like the 'peace and love' groups helped unify the Sixties generation. **1995**

Drugs

Natural fruit juice is great, better'n any drug, gives you a natural sugar rush. 1985

How would I have kept this together for so long if I was on drugs? It'd be impossible. You could not do what I have done if you were into drugs. I mean, I used a few drugs. I smoked a lot of grass in the Sixties, continued to smoke grass into the Seventies and dabbled around in other drugs. But I never got hooked on... you know, never got out of hand with the harder drugs. I experimented, but I think I'm basically a survivor. I've never been an alcoholic. Never used heroin.

There was never any heroin directly around me, 'cause people knew how I felt about it. Anything that killed people, I didn't want to have. Anything that you had to have, that was bigger than you, I'm not for that. **1988**

I was fried for *The Last Waltz*. I was on my way out, falling on stage, and someone said, "Here, have some of this," I'd been up for two days, so I had some. And I was gone, you know? I'm not proud of it; I don't think people should see that and think, "Wow, that's cool."

When they were editing the film, they asked me if I wanted to have that removed. And Robbie Robertson said, "The way you are is kinda like what the whole movie's about – if you keep on doin' this, you're just gonna die, so we're going to stop doing it." They just caught me at a bad time. I had been on the road for forty-five days, and I'd done two shows the night before in Atlanta, and I just got carried away, and we just blew it out the window. So I was still up. But I don't do that anymore. I'm one of the lucky ones who was able to do that and able to stop. But it wasn't that easy to stop that lifestyle. I had to spend some time. The monster kept coming back every once in a while. I could stop for three or four weeks or a couple of months, then I'd get back into it, just for one or two nights, then I'd stop again. It took a long time. I don't even know if it's over now. 1988

I haven't smoked any (grass) since October 7. The main reason is that on October 7 Elliot Roberts, my manager, called and told me that it looked like I was going to get off Geffen Records. And I had just smoked this big bomber, and I almost had a heart attack. I was so happy, but I was too high to enjoy it. So I stopped. I just didn't have my senses, my faculties together enough to enjoy the moment. **1988**

I'm concerned for my children, particularly my eldest son. He has to face 'drugs' every day in the school yard, drugs that are way stronger than anything I got offered in most of my years as a professional musician.

I've got to say right here, I think 'drugs' from my experience are beatable. Drugs are transitory. The environment's a whole different issue. We've simply got to come to terms with the fact that we've done damage to the world that we may not be able to undo. We've got to try and save this planet. I mean, compared to that reality, 'drugs' are really... just drugs. 1990

Rock'n'roll is like a drug... I don't want to do it all the time 'cos it'll kill me. **1990**

Rock'n'roll's a drug-fuelled music... but there's a lot of different drugs. And a drug doesn't necessarily have to be a chemical substance so much as a metaphor for something that stimulates you, that charges you up. For me now, physical training is like a drug. I do that to get 'charged up'. It works too... mostly.

At the same time, drugs as chemical substances, I still find very threatening. I've had a thing for drugs but I don't think that it's scarred me. I'm just scarred by life. Nothing in particular... Only other people often don't let themselves know how damaged they are, like I do, and deal with it. 1990

I got burnt out somewhere around Albuquerque (in 1966). I just collapsed basically. We'd met a bunch of hippies and ended up crashing in their 'pad'. I slept for a couple of days, then went to the hospital for exhaustion. They told me to eat, sleep and rest – the usual.

In retrospect, I'm really not sure what it was that kept me up for so long. I'm not sure if any chemicals were involved. **1995**

Politics

Jimmy Carter

In the Carter years, everybody was walking around with their tails between their legs talking with their head down, y'know, thinking America's been so bad, we've done all these things wrong. But, especially militarily, we had a lot of disasters and a lot of things that never should have happened and that maybe were mistakes in the first place, although it's hard to say.

People were being killed everywhere before we went over to try to help, and we went over and tried to help them and we fucked up. But y'know, you can't always feel sorry for everything that you did. Obviously I wish no-one had to die in any war, but war is a dirty game.

It seems like the Soviets, it doesn't bother them that much to walk into Afghanistan and kill people left and right and take the fucking country and do all that shit. You can't just let them keep on doing that without saying enough's enough. So to do that, to have the strength to do that, you have to be strong.

Ten years ago the US was starting to really drag ass, way behind the Soviets in build-up. All that's happened lately is more or less to catch up, just to be equal, reach equality in arms. At best it's a bad situation, but I think it would be worse to be weak when the stronger nation is the aggressor against freedom.

So I stand behind Reagan when it comes to build-up, to stand, be able to play hardball with other countries that are aggressive towards free countries. I don't think there's anything wrong with that.

I wouldn't have thought that in 1967. But I'm an older man now, I have a family. I see other people with families. There's no immediate threat to American families, but there is an immediate threat to other families in free countries, y'know, a lot of the countries on the borders of the Iron Curtain. To stand there and say it could never happen is wrong, because it's happened. We just don't want it to happen any more – at least, I don't. 1985

Ronald Reagan

It (the size of the defence budget) is crazy, it's fucking nuts. At least in our countries we have the fucking freedom to stand up and say it's crazy. And that's what we're fighting for, to be able to disagree. Openly. And it's our right, and we have to do everything we can to preserve it.

So I don't put down anybody who says we should stop building weapons and everything. I disagree with them, practically. Idealistically I agree with them. It's like walking both sides of the fence, but I think there's too much to be responsible for as men and as people, that you have to take care of your own.

So that's why I have more of a sympathy for Reagan than other people would have – a lot of other people in my walk of life. **1985**

**I think it's time to be positive. I think if all the hippies and
everything from the Sixties, if they're still complaining about every
little fucking thing, if they're not happy about anything, it's their
own fucking fault. Cos they're the ones who should have changed it.
Time has gone by now and what we have is what we've done so far,
and if they're still putting down everything that they've done then
I really don't feel compassion for that.**

**We should be proud of the things we have been able to do,
and the positive aspects of who we are in the world. It's our own
creativity, ingenuity, whatever you wanna call it. I don't think all
that's dead in America, I think it's still there. I feel that the Sixties
was a decade of idealism, and the Eighties is more of realism.** 1985

I'm not into organised religion. I'm into believing in a higher
source of creation, realising that we're all just part of nature and
we're all animals. We're very highly evolved and we should be very
responsible for what we've learned. I even go as far as to think that
in the plan of things, the natural plan of things, that the rockets and
the satellites, spaceships, that we're creating now a really… we're
pollinating, as a universe, and it's part of the universe. Earth is a
flower and it's pollinating. It's starting to send out things, and now
we're evolving, they're getting bigger and they're able to go further.
And they have to, because we need to spread out now in
the universe. I think in 100 years we'll be living on other planets.

I'm the same guy I always was. I don't care. Maybe they thought because country music is country music that I was a right-winger. I don't know. The other day some guy asked me if I thought I was a black man because I'm playing the blues. What are you supposed to say? 1988

I became much more involved in family, taking care of the family, making sure the family was secure. And I related to Reagan's original concept of big government and federal programs fading away so that communities could handle their own programs, like day care. That was the crux of his domestic message, and I thought the idea was good. I thought it would bring people together. But it was a real idealistic thing, and people didn't really come together. **1988**

I was very disillusioned with Jimmy Carter. On a political level, I don't think we ever should have given back the Panama Canal. I just have a gut feeling that that was a huge mistake made out of guilt, not out of reasoning. He was going to make up for all the other bad things we'd done in the world by giving back the Panama Canal. I also think it was wrong to have let the armed forces deteriorate to a point where our strength was less than it had been at a time when other superpowers were growing. I just don't think it was good ball playing.
**   I'm not a hawk. I'm not one who wants to go to war and flex muscles and everything, but I just don't believe that you can talk from a weakness. I think it is as straightforward as that. Everybody in the world is playing hardball, and if we say we're not going to play hardball anymore... I don't think it's going to work. People are going to confuse that as weakness and take advantage of it.** 1988

I think Reagan really did want to do the things that he said he wanted to do. I was disappointed in many of the things that happened during his administration. But I thought that the ideas that were behind a lot of the things he tried to do were things that I could relate to. I just couldn't back away from that. **1988**

I would not like to see George Bush as president of the United States. I don't think the former leader of the CIA should be president. We need someone with compassion, someone who has a lot of feelings and a lot of savvy. I think (Jesse) Jackson's the best. He's the guy I would like to see just for interest's sake. I would like to see what would happen, because there would be a lot of change. 1988

My political views are meandering at best. I don't really see much difference between the Republicans and the Democrats; they just tell different stories. **1989**

Now, everybody wants democracy. Now the communists think it might be worth a shot, y'know. I don't want to burst the balloon, but freedom has big problems too.

The Eastern Bloc countries used to say "Look at capitalism, it's sick, these people are all degenerates, there's drugs on the street, there's murders on the street" – that's part of freedom. There's a lot of bad people, and they're free to do almost anything they want until they get caught. So freedom is a two-edged sword. 1989

There are three possibilities as far as I can see for the country. Radical change, change and no change. Clinton's in the middle. He stands for moderate change. Radical change is Ross Perot. And I'm kind of a radical, myself. I think if you're gonna stir things up, stir 'em up hard. Do it, get it done. At the same time, I have to warn myself that some things are too big to move too fast, otherwise you'll break 'em. You can't take a big thing and change it overnight.

Conventional wisdom says that Clinton would be the best bet for president because he won't move so fast. But Ross Perot has a sense of genius about him that I find very interesting. I'm not scared by him. A lot of people find him sinister and threatening. But that's because he's so open. No one's ever seen a politician like this before... And think of the impact he'd have. It would be a radical change on the whole world, the entire global economic structure. It's certainly something to think about.

Clinton's a fighter. I like that about him. He's just trucking along. He never stops coming at you. He's taken a lotta shit, but he's still coming. **1992**

Bill Clinton

The Films

Journey Through The Past was something that I wanted to do. The music, which has been and always will be my primary thing, just seemed to point that way. I wanted to express a visual picture of what I was singing about.

It's hard to say what the movie means. I think it's a good film for a first film. I think it's a really good film. I don't think I was trying to say that life is pointless. It does lay a lot of shit on people, though. It wasn't made for entertainment. I'll admit it, I made it for myself. Whatever it is, that's the way I felt. I made it for me. I never even had a script.

The film community doesn't want to see me in there. What do they want with *Journey Through The Past*? It's got no plot. No point. No stars. They don't want to see that. But the next time, man, we'll get them. The next time. I've got all the equipment, all the ideas and motivation to make another picture. I've even been keeping my chops up as a cameraman by being on hire under the name of Bernard Shakey. I filmed a Hyatt House commercial not too long ago. I'm set. I'm just waiting for the right time. 1975

On the Rust Never Sleeps film in 'Rust-O-Vision'

It enables the audience to see… certain people in the audience,
mind you, not everyone can see this… but everyone should put on the
glasses and give it a shot as far as I can tell… You have to be in the
right state of mind to see rust particles… It's a very high-tech thing.
Few people understand it, actually, but you put on these glasses and at
certain points, especially in the older songs, you can see it and you can
tell where the band starts to falter… With the glasses on while I'm
playing, if you're tuned in you can see it falling all over the floor of
the stage, running down the cord of my guitar… **1979**

**This (*Rust Never Sleeps*) is my second film – probably the first film
most people would notice – and in the future I'd like to do more.**
1979

I had two little video-8 cameras, which I left running all the time.
I would just come into rooms and put them down on the table.
And the point of view (of *Muddy Track*) is really from the camera.
The camera takes on an identity – its name is Otto – and people start
talking to the camera. And this camera saw a lot of things that really
go down on a tour that are not cute or funsy-wunsy. It's not like the
pop-band-on-the-road type of thing. There's a lot of guts in it, a lot
of feeling. **1988**

***Muddy Track* covers a lot of that. Covers that feeling,
you know? There's some wild stuff in there where we do speed
metal. A lot of the music is only the beginnings and ends of songs.
The songs themselves aren't there. It's like the interviews are
only the interviewer. And you hardly ever see me. You only hear
questions. It's an interesting concept of your point of view. And it
talks about what it's like to be forty-one, forty-two, and still be
doing that kind of music.** 1988

My cinematic vision is pretty much all taken from Godard.
He's my main influence, him and certain other *cinéma vérité* guys.
1990

**You'll like this film that I made that's called *Muddy Track*.
That one's a documentary of me and Crazy Horse on the road two
or three years ago. There's a sequence when I filmed all the
interviewers who came to interview me. Then I picked the most
ridiculous questions and didn't answer them.** 1990

That was a bad period for us. We weren't playing well then.
Overall, the material wasn't up to much. I made a film about that tour,
the legendary *Muddy Track* (laughs). I still want the films I directed to
all come out in a special six-pack: *Human Highway*, *Rust Never Sleeps*,
Journey Through The Past...Muddy Track is really my favourite of all
of them, though. It's dark as hell. God, it's a heavy one! But it's funky.
1995

Young On Young

**There's a lot I have to say. I never did interviews because
they always got me in trouble. Always. They never came out right.
I just don't like them. As a matter of fact, the more I didn't do them
the more they wanted them; the more I said by not saying anything.
But things change, you know. I feel very free now. I don't have an
old lady anymore. I relate it a lot to that. I'm back living in Southern
California. I feel more open than I have in a long while. I'm coming
out and speaking to a lot of people. I feel like something new is
happening in my life.** 1975

There was too much going on the last couple of years. None of it
had anything to do with music. I just had too many people hanging
around who don't really know me. They were parasites, whether
they intended to be or not. They lived off me, used my money to buy
things, used my telephone to make their calls. General leeching.

It hurt my feelings a lot when I reached that realisation. I didn't
want to believe I was being taken advantage of. I didn't like having to
be boss, and I don't like having to say, 'Get the fuck out.' That's why
I have different houses now. When people gather around me, I just
split now. I mean, my ranch is more beautiful and lasting than ever.
It's strong without me. I just don't feel like it's the only place I can
be and be safe anymore. I feel much stronger now. **1975**

**People don't understand sometimes how I can come in and
go out so fast. How I can be there and want to do something and
then when it's over, it's over. To other people, it's just beginning.
I've got a job to do. The Eighties are here. I've just got to tear
down whatever has happened to me and build something new.
You can only have it for so long before you don't have it any more.
You become an old-timer... which... I could be... I don't know.** 1979

Any group that comes along and does its thing for three or
four years, unless they change, they go away, they're gone, they're
finished. The fact is, I'm still around because I've changed. **1987**

**Shakey Deal? Well, that's just a nickname. The leader of
The Bluenotes is this crock called Shakey and he's sometimes me.
It's good to have different identities in life. Particularly if you're
me, because I wake up in the morning and don't know who I am
anyway. It often takes me quite a while to work out who I am...**
1988

There's not that many (rock stars) left from where I started off –
but perhaps that's because half of them are dead. That speaks for itself.
But as for why I keep moving... well, punk rock was great because it
woke up all these old cronies like me to the fact that we were just
repeating ourselves until further notice. **1988**

Unfortunately rock has become an establishment again. It's a
bore, actually. Once it gets like that it's not really happening, it's not
the essence of rock'n'roll. I try so hard not to be part of the rock
establishment but I guess I am just because I've been around so long.
To be an 'elder statesman of rock'n'roll' or whatever is such a bore.
The only thing in this country which seems to be breaking new
ground is some of the really radical bands like Anthrax and Metallica.
They give young kids an expression and kids know their parents
hate them – turn that fucking noise down – so they can relate to it.
So if I was 18 again I'd be in a metal band, not playing the blues for
the old folks. That's what rock'n'roll's good for: it's a sound of
revenge. **1988**

**Money is nice but it's not necessary. But money is nice for
your old age. Because look at me – I'm fucking falling apart.
I'm constantly corroding. If you stand still that's when it really gets
you. Take a look at some of those steel buildings that have been
there for a long time, they're just corroding. It's like a warning to
me. Stay still, Shakey, and you'll turn to rust and dust. So I keep
on moving...** 1988

Michael Jackson's just trying to cop my shit. *I* was insane *years* ago...
1988

**I've got a few demons, but I manage to co-exist with them.
The demons are there all the time y'know, that's what makes you
crazy, that's what makes me play my guitar the way I play it
sometimes. Depends on the balance, how strong the demons are
that night, how strong the good is. There's always a battle between
good and evil in every second in your life, I think. In every
judgement you make both sides are represented in your mind.
You may hide the bad side, but it's there.**

I had a great time. I think a lot of us had a great time back then.
But I don't see myself as being stuck in the Sixties or anything like
that – except that I still have long hair. **1988**

**It's just the way I am. When I was in school, I would go for
six months wearing the same kind of clothes. Then all of a sudden
I'd wear all different clothes. It's change. It's always been like
that.** 1988

The question is, how long can you keep doing it? And really be
doing it? Or do you become a re-enactment of an earlier happening?
That's a question I ask myself. **1988**

**I could feel it starting to slip away. And I never wanted to be in
front of people and have them pay to see me when I'm not 100 per
cent there. And if you feel that energy slipping away, then you've
got to fold your deck, you know, get out.** 1988

I guess I'm pretty extreme in myself. I've run the gauntlet of emotions quite a bit in my life; things have happened to me that have been extreme in response. There's anger in everything I do and sometimes it's so understated that it's almost like a pretty thing. Anger is only a bad thing if you can't control it. My life is completely out of control but my wildness mostly comes out in the music. **1989**

I'm happy when I'm on the road because I control everything that goes on around me and I feel secure because I know what's going to happen. But with the last show, you're in limbo. The show's over and you're only as good as the last note you played. It's like you're in an aeroplane and you go through the sound barrier and you're going faster and faster and it's all great, everything's working fine. Then suddenly, the plane's gone and you're still up there. That's what it feels like to end a tour.

But, hey, I love to play; that's what I do. As long as I keep landing, I'll be able to go up there again. There's a tribute album to me out right now *The Bridge* and I love those people and it's nice that they did that but I'm not ready for that. They don't mean to close the book but to me it's still threatening. 1989

I keep changing. Whatever I feel like doing, I try to do. I don't try to do what I did. **1989**

The first thing you have to understand about me is that no one tells me what to do. It's just not gonna work. I'm not gonna listen, simple as that.

What I'm saying here, I guess, is that I don't give a damn. Never have. Never will. I do what I do and I always have done. It's all I can do. I can't do anything else. And a lot of the time over the last ten years, I know what I've done hasn't been the kind of thing that people wanted from me. It hasn't been the Neil Young that people wanted to hear.

I had to battle every time I went out. It was an uphill battle with every album, from the beginning to the end. I was fighting the record company, I was fighting general reactions to what I was doing that weren't really all that encouraging. Still, what I was doing was what I wanted to do. So I did it. And what I did, it wasn't what people wanted from me. And I knew that... At the same time, I couldn't give them what they wanted, so it didn't really bother me. 1990

I know that some people are convinced that I've spent the last ten years systematically destroying my career, taking this music that my audience thought was so super-valuable it shouldn't even be touched, taking it and ruining it.

But you have to do that sometimes, however painful it is. It clears the horizon and gives you a new beginning. You can't stand still. You don't stop, ever. If you stop, you're dead. You know, what I am, I'm a musician. I'm not a superstar. I'm a musician. That's what I am. I'm a writer and a musician. The more I play, the more different things I do, the better I get at what I do.

I'm not gonna grow if I'm just giving people what they think they want to hear from me. I'm not gonna grow sitting in a mansion. I'm gonna die. And I don't want to do that. So I keep going out there. And I don't care what people think. I just want to keep going. I want to keep the blood flowing… Hell, that's my job. **1990**

I don't mind dying. I don't mind getting old. But I don't wanna be passive about it. I'm not gonna go quietly, you know. I'm not gonna just wander off, and they're not gonna take me off quietly.

I'll tell you something, when I go, I'm gonna go fighting. That's for sure. 1990

I'm a shadow of my former self. I know it. But there's nothing I can do about it. And anyway, I kind of like it that way. **1990**

It's all running away. I've been running all my life. Where I'm going… who the fuck knows? But that's not the point. 1990

I was pretty down I guess at the time (of *On The Beach*), but I just did what I wanted to do… I think if everybody looks back at their own lives they'll realise that they went through something like that. There's periods of depression, periods of elation, optimism and scepticism, the whole thing… it just keeps coming in waves. You go down to the beach and watch the same thing, just imagine every wave is a different set of emotions coming in. Just keep coming. As long as you don't ignore it, it'll still be there.

If you start shutting yourself off and not letting yourself live through the things that are coming through you, I think that's when people start getting old really fast, that's when they really age. 'Cos they decide that they're happy to be what they were at a certain time in their lives when they were happiest, and they say 'that's where I'm gonna be for the rest of my life'. From that moment on they're dead, y'know, just walking around to avoid that. **1988**

I spend most of my time trying to remain open to new things. They reflect the fact that I've got so interested in electronics and machines. I've always loved machines. I feel that with all the new digital and computerised equipment I can get my hands on now, I can do things I could never do before… I know this is just the beginning for me. I've been Neil Young for years and I could stay where I am and be a period piece but as I look around everything's so organised…the new music with its kind of perfection is reassuring for me… the manipulation of machines can be very soulful. 1988

Right now there is no end. I mean, the only end is the *big* end. Okay? I can keep going for a long time... **1990**

I'm tired of the treadmill, the summer sheds (amphitheatres). I'm playing the shitholes from now on. I loved the Boston Garden. It almost fell down when we played there last time. And the guy was so happy to see us back! I want to play those old places while they're still there... That's my new motto – 'Shove the sheds!' 1991

I haven't given people what they want all the time, so therefore they haven't come to expect anything from me that I can let them down on. It's because I basically follow myself. I'm not bored at all with what I'm doing. Some people like to make records but they don't want to play live. I like to do both. **1992**

I went as far as I could with grunge but I love it and I'll do it again some day. When I played the Bob Fest (Dylan's 30th anniversary show) I got out my electric guitar and amp, dusted 'em down and it felt good. Before I went on to play, I was down below sharing a dressing room with Eric Clapton, listening through the walls until my number came up. I couldn't wait to get on stage. 1993

I've just discovered that the way to make music for me is just to make it when it's really trying to come out. That's when I drop everything else and call whoever I need to call to get it together, whoever I can get at the time. It's more important to get it than it is to have my crew or my people or anything like that. It's important to just grab the moment and go for it. **1995**

Well, I have been singing the same song for 30 years. I really have. Now I'm old enough, I look at it and it does seem like one big song and I just play different parts of it.

    I was in danger of self-parody in 1969 with my second record. But, y'know, I got a good track record of not being a self-parody... unless your viewpoint of me is that I am. And then, of course, I've been doing it for years! 1995

Rock'n'roll should never die. It should just keep on going. And I'm there. I'm having a good time. **1995**

One day Neil Young will write a happy song. But I'll probably sell it to TV for a commercial.

There are several records like *On The Beach* and *Time Fades Away*. See, that's something you have to understand: I don't make a habit of listening to my old stuff. Ever. I listened to *Weld* once since I finished it. *Freedom* I've heard once. I spend so much time making them that when it's over, I just never want to listen to 'em again. I just send 'em out into the world like an evil father... **1995**

With Eddie Vedder

I just work out a lot. Make sure I stay in good shape. If you'll notice, I'm not exactly that skinny-looking guy from the Sixties and Seventies any more. I weight over 40 pounds more than I used to back then. And none of it is fat – it's all muscle. 1995

On his epilepsy

Epilepsy is something nobody knows much about. It's just a part of me. Part of my head, part of what's happening in there. Sometimes something in my brain triggers it off. Sometimes when I get really high, it's a very psychedelic experience to have a seizure. You slip into some other world. Your body's flapping around and you're biting your tongue and battering your head on the ground, but your mind is off somewhere else. The only scary thing about it is not going or being there; it's realising you're totally comfortable in this...*void*. And that shocks you back into reality. It's a very disorienting experience. It's difficult to get a grip on yourself. The last time it happened, it took about an hour and a half of just walking around the ranch with two of my friends to get it together.

It never has (happened on stage). I felt like it a couple of times, and I've always left the stage. I get too high or something. It's just pressure from around, you know. That's why I don't like crowds too much. **1975**

Now when it happens, I can control it. I don't know whether I just couldn't control it or whether there just weren't too many new things happening to me. Whatever it was, I'd just get this feeling inside of me and I'd just go...! Now, when I get that feeling, I'll lay back or turn off everything. Close off the input for a while. It's a little hard to do that when you're on stage in front of a lot of people. Although I still do it. I haven't had any 'events' for almost 20 years. None of any real consequence anyway. But I have had... y'know, 'tremors'. I sense it's still there. 1995

On his epitaph

This man, the longest living rock'n'roll star, died searching for a heart of gold. He never found it, but he turned a few people on. **1975**

The Critics

I don't care what they (critics) call me. It means very little.
People are always tearing me apart but if I'm weird it's because
I *want* to be weird. If the yuppie point of view is that I'm a weirdo,
what the hell does *that* mean? People write in magazines that
I make different records just to draw attention to myself. If I ever
saw the little wimps that were saying that then I'm sure that
I'd have to fucking *kill* them. What kind of thing is that to say?
There's many better ways to draw attention to *myself*. I could kill
music critics if I wanted to and that would get a lot of attention.
I could be on the news. I could have burned down Geffen Records.
I could have been on the news. I could have got a lot of attention.
I could burn myself down in public if I wanted to – that would
get a lot of attention, right?

It's a very stupid thing to assume that I'm making different
kinds of music to draw attention to myself... What are these guys
saying? Are they saying that the cool thing to do is to just the same
thing over and over again and not be a weirdo? Is that what they
are saying? Because if Neil Young *did* do the same thing over and
over again and *wasn't* a weirdo, then these guys would be going
'Oh, Neil Young, he's so boring coming out with the same thing over
and over and over again'. You can't win. You know, one week I'm
a jerk and the next week I'm a genius, so how can I take these
music critics seriously? Let the people decide.

These critics don't bother me... but they sure bother my
mother. She saw the review of my album in *Rolling Stone* and
they had this drawing, this cartoon of me and it didn't look like me
and I had three arms and my mother called me up and said, 'What
happened? Did you get plastic surgery? Are you trying to be like
Michael Jackson now? 1988

When people think that I'm just doing this on a whim, it discounts the music. Music is immediate to me. It's something that's happening right now, and it's a reflection of what's going on with the people who are making it. It has nothing to do with what they did or what they are going to do.

You know, I used to be pissed off at Bobby Darin because he changed styles so much. Now I look at him and I think he was a fucking genius. I mean, from 'Queen Of The Hop' to 'Mack The Knife'. Dig that. And it didn't mean that he didn't believe in 'Queen Of The Hop' when he turned around and did a Frank Sinatra thing.

Yet I come up against this because I experiment around and I play different kinds of music. In my eyes, it doesn't make what I'm doing any less valid. **1988**

I saw the 'inside' of the hard journalism business when he (writer father Scott Young) would take me to the office when I was just a kid. I saw how a story could be manipulated. I never trusted it then and I don't trust it now. I never believed 'em when they said I'd made a bad album. Why should I believe them when they say I've got a good one? 1990

I got a terrible reaction when I played those songs (*Harvest*) live. The critics didn't like 'em, but the songs have endured for years so I don't know what criteria they use. But there's a certain honour to be trashed. It's like redemption. **1993**

I've had a good time. And even when people didn't particularly like what I was doing, which I can tell because people don't buy it and don't go to see you – it was still a challenge that was rewarding. It's always fun to do what you feel like doing and watch the things change around you. 1995

David Briggs (producer) told me what was wrong with my performance at Bob-Aid. Everyone else was telling me how great it was. He didn't belabour the fact that it was great. His opinion was: "Yeah, it was great, OK. It was great *but* forget about that because what was wrong was… this, this and this. You sang it in the wrong key, your voice was too low, the drums weren't tight enough 'til half-way through… No-one'll probably notice but… it's not usable."
And I always listen to what he has to say and take note of it. **1995**

We get on great now but, at a certain point, Jack (Nitzsche) made a call on me that I had copped/sold out. Maybe it was something I did in the early Seventies, during *Harvest* or *Goldrush* – I don't know when exactly it happened, but somewhere along the line it happened. It was his opinion that I wasn't living up to my potential even at that early stage. He was one of the guys who could see how fucked up I was compared to what I could really do. He was one of my earliest critics. He was a trailblazer in that respect. 1995

Onstage with Bob Dylan at the Bobfest, the concert at New Yorks Madison Square Garden, to celebrate the 30th Anniversary of the release of Dylan's first record

Geffen Records

David Geffen

Oh, yeah, 'uncharacteristic' material. But what's *this*, what's
The Bluenotes – this is *very* uncharacteristic what I'm doing now, right?
And I wouldn't have even been able to make this record on Geffen.
I definitely would have had to have paid for the whole thing myself –
which I did. I made this record when I didn't have a record company.
This Note's For You is totally my own thing. I did it after Geffen and
I brought it to Reprise with me and it's the first record I've ever made
without the interference of a record company in seven or eight years.
But with that law suit, eventually they (Geffen Records) dropped it
after a year and a half of harassing me because I told them the longer
you sue for playing country music, the longer I'm going to play country
music. Either you back off or I'm going to play country music forever.
And then you won't be able to sue me anymore because country music
will be what I always do so it won't be 'uncharacteristic' anymore,
hahaha. So stop telling me what to do or I'll turn into George Jones.
So finally David Geffen called me up one day and said, "I'm wrong.
This was the wrong thing to do. I'm sorry. We shouldn't have done it
and it didn't work. I was wrong." And I said, "Too right you're wrong."
I don't know what he was thinking of. It was a pretty weird situation…
It's quite a distinction, though, to be sued for not being commercial
after making hit records for 20 years. **1988**

**They (Geffen Records) had a very negative viewpoint of
anything that I wanted to do, other than straight pop records that
were exactly what they wanted to hear. They saw me as a product
that was not living up to their expectations. They didn't see me
as an artist.** 1988

There was a whole other record, the original *Old Ways*, which
Geffen rejected. It was like *Harvest II*. It was a combination of the
musicians from *Harvest* and *Comes A Time*. It was done in Nashville in
only a few days, basically the same way Harvest was done, and it was
co-produced by Elliot Mazer, who produced *Harvest*.
    There's *Harvest*, *Comes A Time* and *Old Ways I*, which is more
of a Neil Young record than *Old Ways II*. *Old Ways II* was more of a
country record – which was a direct result of being sued for playing
country music. The more they tried to stop me, the more I did it.
Just to let them know that no-one's gonna tell me what to do.
    I was so stoked about that record. I sent them a tape of it
that had eight songs on it. I called them up a week later, 'cause I hadn't
heard anything, and they said, 'Well, frankly, Neil, this record scares us
a lot. We don't think this is the right direction for you to be going in.'
The technopop thing was happening, and they had Peter Gabriel, and
they were totally into that kind of trip. I guess they just saw me as
some old hippie from the Sixties still trying to make acoustic music or
something… **1988**

It's hard for me to disassociate the frustrations that I had during that period (Geffen Records) from the actual works I was able to create. I really tried to do my best during that period, but I felt that I was working under duress.

In all my time at Warner Bros, they never cancelled a session. For any reason. And it happened several times at Geffen. It was blatant manipulation. It was just so different from anything I'd ever experienced.

They buried *Everybody's Rockin'*. They did less than nothing. They decided, 'That record's not gonna get noticed. We're gonna press as few of those as possible and not do anything.'

There was another record of mine, called *Island In The Sun*, which will probably never be heard. It was the first record I made for Geffen. The three acoustic songs on *Trans* are from it. But they advised me not to put it out. Because it was my first record for Geffen, I thought, 'Well, this is a fresh, new thing. He's got some new ideas.' It didn't really register to me that I was being manipulated. Until the second record. Then I realised this is the way it is all the time. Whatever I do, it's not what they want. 1988

Geffen was just a mis-match. It was a bad marriage. It just didn't work out. And it got to be a personal thing. It was a bad deal. But they're a great company. They're an efficient organisation. They've got some great groups, and they've sold a lot of records. Unfortunately, none of them were mine. **1990**

We went through a lot of changes when (David Geffen) managed Crosby Stills Nash & Young and when he signed me in the Eighties he didn't seem to comprehend how… uh, diverse my musical career would become. So he took it personally when I handed him a straight country album or a rockabilly album. He thought I was making those albums to laugh at him, as a joke at his expense. 1990

Actually, it's funny: R.E.M. were going to go with Geffen, then they heard I was being sued and everything, they just dropped all contact with Geffen and signed with Warner Bros instead. Geffen actually lost R.E.M. simply for suing me over *Everybody's Rockin'*! **1995**